An Embattled and Unapologetic Liberal

An Embattled and Unapologetic Liberal

Selected Opinion Editorials and Commentaries of G. Alan Hickrod

with assistance from Gwen B. Pruyne

iUniverse, Inc.

New York Lincoln Shanghai

An Embattled and Unapologetic Liberal
Selected Opinion Editorials and Commentaries of G. Alan Hickrod

iUniverse books may be ordered through booksellers or by contacting:

iUniverse
2021 Pine Lake Road, Suite 100
Lincoln, NE 68512
www.iuniverse.com
1-800-Authors (1-800-288-4677)

ISBN-13: 978-0-595-36861-7 (pbk)
ISBN-13: 978-0-595-81272-1 (ebk)
ISBN-10: 0-595-36861-1 (pbk)
ISBN-10: 0-595-81272-4 (ebk)

Printed in the United States of America

Royalties from this book go to the Hubbard-Hickrod Scholarship, administered by the Illinois State University Foundation and the Department of Educational Administration, College of Education, ISU. This fund supports graduate students in Educational Administration and is not political in nature.

Independent contributions to this scholarship, in addition to these royalties, are both encouraged and appreciated. Mail to Illinois State University Foundation, Campus Box 8000, Normal, Illinois 61790-8000.

Dedication

This book is dedicated to my wife, Dr. Marcia Escott Hickrod, who understands that even an elderly, retired professor still has some things he must say. It is also dedicated to my stepdaughter, Beth Escott Newcomer, who knows that writing is a compulsion, as well as a profession. It is also dedicated to my granddaughter, Hazel Jane Valle Escott. Hazel, I wish I had won more wars for you, but, when you are old enough, you can read this book and know that I tried.

It is also dedicated to all the members of the Huang and Liu Families, whom my late wife, Professor Lucy Jen Huang Hickrod, brought to the United States. Huang Jen Wha was a strong, liberal Democrat who voted in every election from the date of her naturalization to just months before her death, when she voted with assistance on an absentee ballot. Should any of you say, "My vote does not count," she is apt to rise from her grave to haunt you. If she does not, I certainly will.

GAH

Contents

Preface

I have known Alan Hickrod for many years as a Distinguished Professor of Education at Illinois State University and as a good friend with whom I frequently exchange views about American and British politics and, occasionally, Scottish politics. Politically, he is a man of the Liberal tradition, under which America grew to be a great country committed to providing opportunities and security to all its people.

He calls himself "a garden-variety liberal," tracing his views back to Franklin Delano Roosevelt's New Deal, Harry Truman's Fair Deal, John F. Kennedy's New Frontier, and Lyndon Johnson's Great Society. These labels began as campaign slogans, but they came to represent the distinctive problems that each of those presidents faced and the distinctive ways in which American Liberalism was adapted to deal with them. He mentions other Liberal politicians whom he admires, especially Hubert Humphrey and Illinois' own Adlai Stevenson and Paul Simon. He spells out his views of Liberalism today in his essay "On A Definition of a Liberal." He notes that the Republican Party also had a liberal tradition as represented by Theodore Roosevelt and Nelson Rockefeller until it was swept aside by Presidents Ronald Reagan and George W. Bush.

Hickrod's Liberalism rests upon a premise that goes back to Aristotle: the importance of a strong middle class to maintain freedom and stability in the state. An aristocracy of great wealth (plutocracy) is a threat to freedom. A large, desperately poor lower class is a threat to stability. The middle class provides balance: it needs freedom to develop its potential and has a powerful interest in maintaining a stable, nurturing society. Hickrod makes clear his alarm at the growth of plutocracy in America and the shrinkage of the middle class. He does not hesitate to identify this problem as the result of "Reaganism" as advocated by the current Republican Party and carried out by President George W. Bush.

In this collection of essays and columns, published over a period of five years in a variety of publications, Hickrod shows how his concern for public education and school finance grew naturally out of the liberal commitment to equal opportunity. He is a nationally recognized authority on public school finance; therefore, the third cluster of essays consists of papers written on that subject. These essays are more interesting than one might at first expect. They provide an introduction to a policy issue that remains with us today and communicate valuable insights into the politics of education in Illinois. Two principal themes emerge. The first is Hickrod's concern for equity in school funding as one aspect of creating a more equitable society. The other is the importance of strong federal and state roles in the funding of schools to overcome the limitations and inequities of schools dependent on local property taxes. Most of these essays deal with Illinois, but they are applicable to schools across the country.

His essay entitled "The Privatization of Education: A Mistake" is typical of his approach to school funding. He concedes that large expenditures for schools in low-income districts may not produce equivalent improvements in educational outcomes, but he justifies them as necessary to level the playing field. He opposes reliance on private schools, which would only increase inequalities of income in the United States "and would ultimately destroy the middle class, replacing it with large concentrations of rich and poor." The public schools, he continues, "provide the glue that holds this conglomerate society together." They contribute to "the upward mobility needed in a democracy," he says, citing De Tocqueville and Lord Acton as foreign visitors who recognized the importance of the American system of public schools. He points out the need for a large, well-educated working class in an advanced economy and the demands of our military services for well-educated personnel.

The key essay is his "Tribute to Ben Hubbard," which recounts the Herculean efforts of his friend and colleague at Illinois State University "to increase the opportunities of poor kids in poor districts." Hubbard worked tirelessly and with considerable success with the Illinois General Assembly, a legislative body not noted for its openness to ideas that would upset the status quo. Hickrod notes that he, too, was involved in these efforts.

The remaining essays testify to Hickrod's wide-ranging interests and the consistency with which he understands them within the framework of American Liberalism. He comments on many of the leaders and great public issues of our time. In the process, he reveals tantalizing tidbits about his personal life: influential professors at Wabash College, service in the Marine Corps, experiences as a graduate student at Harvard, and his interest in Scotland, the British Liberal Party, and the Masons. He acknowledges the influence of the works of John Kenneth Galbraith, Louis Hartz, Arthur M. Schlesinger Jr., Karl Popper, and Paul Simon.

In a collection of essays written over a period of time, it is inevitable that certain ideas and phrases will be repeated. Remarkably, these repetitions are not annoying, but actually enhance the essays. The fact that most of them represent responses to concrete issues located in a specific time and place lends them freshness. They show how a thoughtful mind, confronted with a multiplicity of problems, will always recur to core principles.

Earl A. Reitan
Normal IL 61761.

Acknowledgments

Books that are written later in one's life cause one to see more clearly all the people who have helped along the way. Only some of these are noted here.

To the late Charles Benson of Harvard University and later the University of California at Berkeley, I am indebted for showing me the larger public policy aspects of School Finance.

To the late John Frederick Charles and the late Byron Trippet of Wabash College, I am indebted for showing me the uses of the past.

The late Colonel Charles Finch helped me to understand the dimensions of the Iraq war.

To my colleague at Illinois State University: Dr. Ramesh Chaudhari, through his careful and detailed quantitative studies, helped me understand the complex structure of educational finance. My long-time friend and collaborator, Distinguished Professor Emeritus Ben Hubbard, taught me a lot about the practical politics of education. Recent books published by Professor of History Emeritus Earl Reitan encouraged me to think that I could publish a work of this nature. Professor Reitan also read the entire manuscript (as did Dr. Marcia Escott Hickrod) and kindly provided a Preface to the work. Mrs. Gwen Pruyne helped me put the material in readable form. This invaluable service she has provided for over a quarter of a century.

Former State Representative Gene Hoffman (Republican) and former State Senators Art Berman (Democrat) and especially John

Maitland (Republican) also contributed to my understanding of Illinois politics.

Beth Escott Newcomer of Escott Associates in Malibu, California, provided the cover and artwork for the publication. Chad Jones of Normal, Illinois, provided the photography.

Finally, to Bill Wills, Editorial Page Editor at the *Pantagraph*, and to Ed Pyne, Editor of the *Normalite*, I am indebted for accepting many of these items for publication in their newspapers.

Introduction

After I retired from Illinois State University in 1997, I took a sabbatical from writing. However, by about 2000, I began to feel that I might have something yet to say about public policy. For more than thirty years, I had published in the field of School Finance. Many of those publications are still available through ERIC and through the web pages of the Department of Educational Administration and Foundations at Illinois State University. I still have some things to say about School Finance so the reader will find some contributions on that score in this book. However, they are of the broader policy nature and not the empirical quantitative works that I once directed toward other professional educators and the Illinois General Assembly.

After retirement, I returned to my habit of reading broadly in the fields of History, Political Science, Economics and Sociology. Based on that reading, I felt that I needed to say something about current public policy matters. Thus, I began to write for two newspapers in McLean County, Illinois, the *Pantagraph* and the *Normalite*. Many of the selections in this book have appeared as either letters to the editor or as commentaries in these papers. Other compositions are published here for the first time.

Why bother to pull all this stuff together? First, for the last five years, I have grown sick and tired of the bad mouthing of the term "Liberal." A large number of people apparently cannot distinguish between "liberal" and "libertine." Granted, Conservatives often feel that the other side is guilty of "rum, romance, and rebellion"; but one would think that a majority of people would understand that Liberalism constitutes an organized and systematic way of looking at the body politic.

Fortunately, there are many fine books on Liberalism, including one by my long-time friend and colleague, Professor Earl Reitan, a fellow citizen of Normal, Illinois. I have noted some of these books in the references at the end of this volume. No matter how many books there are out there though, it is apparent that lots of folks have not gotten the message.

The second reason is that Liberals have been an embattled minority for the last two decades at the national level and for many years longer than that at selected regional and local levels. In McLean County, Illinois, for example, the normal voting pattern is about 60 percent Republican to 40 percent Democrat. That same ratio prevails across many counties in Illinois and Indiana. It is true that some of those Republican votes could be described as "Liberal," although they prefer usually to describe themselves as "Progressive." However, the progressive wing of the Republican Party has been shrinking since 1980.

These local areas, often as a result of re-districting, translate into "safe" legislative districts at both the state and national levels. The political discourse in these areas tends to be directed toward the "base" of the political parties. That is, the Conservatives and the Liberals tend to talk to themselves rather than to each other. The Conservatives feel they have no need to gather further votes, they already have a large majority, while the Liberals become disheartened through years, indeed decades, of being in a permanent minority status. This breaks down the dialectic. There is no thesis and antithesis presented; therefore, no synthesis can take place. "Safe" districts are the bane of American political life. This little book is not going to solve this gigantic problem, but it at least may start more discussion flowing across party lines.

Additionally, this is not a "neo-liberal" book. It is just a plain, ordinary, garden-variety liberal book. Some may well think it an "unreconstructed New Deal Democrat" book. Maybe it is even a "paleo-liberal" effort. It is certainly true that I do think that the Democratic Party would be well advised to look to its roots and return to many of its prior public policy positions. As Paul Starr has recently said in celebrating the establishment of the premier Liberal journal, *The American Prospect*, some fifteen years ago: "The more fundamental the challenge Liberals face, the greater is the need to explain the grounds of liberal commitments and to give Americans good reasons to make those commitments their own."

I have some confidence that the book will be well received because the items in the local newspapers have been, on the whole, well received. I have always been most encouraged by life-long Republicans who have found at least some positions here that they could also accept. This tells me that, at some level, the dialectic is still working.

Since these essays were written as newspaper pieces, each one intended to stand on its own, there is some repetition of themes and phraseology. I have not attempted to edit all of that out. If the theme is repeated, it is because I consider it important and want the reader to consider it important. With a few exceptions, the essays are either nearly 350 words in length or nearly 800 words in length, those being the dimensions required by the newspapers. Many times, I felt these limits burdensome; but, in reflection, I think they were good for me. At least, they made me work toward that old Scottish Gaelic maxim: "Na abair ach beagan agus abair gu math e." (Say but little and say that well.)

I learned a long time ago that, in matters of political economy, public finance, and educational finance there is no absolute truth. You just make your best case and let other people make theirs. Therefore, if you would like to take issue with anything I have said here by all means send me your comments to the e-mail address listed below.

GAH, Normal, Illinois
AlanHickrod@aol.com
Summer, 2005

Section I

"Liberalism, which seeks what it considers to be an improvement or progress, necessarily desires to change the existing order."

—Columbia Encyclopedia, Sixth Edition

I. Liberalism and Governmental Reform

On a Definition of a Liberal

[Editorial Note: For a further treatment of this subject, see the special issue of *The American Prospect* of June 2005.]

In our "sound bites" mentality, we routinely slam around labels like, "right wing" and "left wing" and "liberal" and "conservative" without realizing that those labels carry very few common understandings. Hence, they do not facilitate rational political discussion. It has not always been so. The late Barry Goldwater wrote, *Conscience of a Conservative*, and millions read the book; by no means, were all of them conservative. Similarly, the late Hubert Humphrey wrote essays in *The American Scholar*, defining what he thought Liberalism meant in the 20th Century; thousands read them; not all of them were Liberals. Since no one else seems to be stepping up to the plate to do similar service for the readers of the *Pantagraph*, perhaps it falls on the shoulders of a retired Illinois State University professor to take a swing at it. At least, I will attempt it here for the liberal side and leave it to a more qualified individual to do it for the conservative side.

There must be a score of points on which one could hang a definition of Liberal as we enter the 21st Century. Only twelve of these public policy positions will be discussed. Some of these policy positions have a range of opinions attached to them. I will try to indicate that variation.

The social security system passed by a liberal president, Franklin Delano Roosevelt, is a bedrock issue for most Liberals. Most Liberals today would support expansion of that program and would be suspicious of attempts to privatize this program since the privatization of the program would not likely benefit Americans of modest circumstances.

The Medicare program passed by another liberal president, Lyndon Baines Johnson, is a second bedrock issue for Liberals. Most Liberals would support expansion of that program to include prescription drug benefits and would support expansion of Medicaid, as well. There is a range of opinion here extending from simple expansion of Medicare through a complete revamping of the way we finance health care in the United States.

Protection of the environment is a strong issue with Liberals and has also been an issue with presidents like Theodore Roosevelt, who would have been more comfortable with the label "progressive." This issue extends into finding substitutions for fossil fuels and into wider issues such as global warming and global over-population.

Some modest redistribution of income is on the agenda of Liberals, although it may be nothing more than a defense of the progressive and graduated income tax and a similar defense of the estate or inheritance tax. There is an important assumption here that should be made explicit. Many Liberals believe that if the private enterprise system is allowed to run unchecked and unregulated, it will result in unequal distribution of wealth. While some variation in wealth is surely justified, given the differences in talent and application among individuals, Liberals often believe that huge inequalities in wealth are not healthful to a representative form of government. In fact, they hold, with Aristotle, that democracies cannot survive great inequalities in wealth. In the Third Book of the *Politics*, Aristotle states that only a large middle class can contribute to the stability of a Republic. Most Liberals accept that as gospel.

Liberals often believe that a more modest defense budget is required than those who are on the other side of the aisle believe. However, the range of opinion here is not as great as one might expect. Surely, there are Liberals who are pacifists. However, until and unless Christianity succeeds with its message of peace on earth, we will need an adequate defense force. Most Liberals see that in terms of a smaller, highly mobile force rather than in terms of a larger "star wars defense." It is not inconsistent, for example, to argue for a four division Marine Corps and still maintain a liberal position. Smaller, elite, rapid deployment units seem to fit our world of "pocket wars," bombings, terrorism and assassinations.

Consistent with point four, Liberals also see the need for rigorous enforcement of anti-trust legislation in order to maintain fair competition in the economy. Similarly, they are apt to stress enforcement of regulations in finance and banking intended to protect the small investor in the economy and to lessen "insider trading." Selected tax breaks for small businesses are consistent with a liberal position, but across the board tax relief for the wealthy is not.

Liberals are strong supporters of public education. They accept the Jeffersonian position that the Republic cannot survive without a well-educated electorate. They are suspicious of proposals to privatize the system through voucher proposals and alternative school proposals, although here the range is quite large. Some Liberals see a role for "charter schools," if they will help the situation of the urban poor and not be restricted simply to the wealthier suburbs. Consistent with their strong support of equal educational opportunity, Liberals are offended by great differences in expenditure per pupil between school districts. They generally support more state aid to school districts and would prefer to depend less upon property taxes to support public education. In higher education, Liberals usually take a low tuition or no tuition stance at least for undergraduate education. The recent success of the Scottish Liberal Democrats in entirely removing tuition at the undergraduate level stands in stark contrast to the increasing tuition levels in U.S. colleges and universities.

Liberals support the separation of Church and State. They view with some fear what they believe to be a lack of religious tolerance among some fundamentalists, both Christian and Muslim. In particular, the attempt of some of these religious groups to impose their will upon the public schools is a cause of some concern. There may be more agnostics, Unitarians, and Reformed Jews in the liberal pews than on the other side of the aisle, but Liberals are also found in ethical organizations like the

Masonic Lodge, largely because that organization has historically stood for religious liberty.

Gun control advocates are more strongly represented among the liberal group than elsewhere in the society. The range here is quite wide. Some Liberals merely work for the registration of all handguns. Others would urge us to follow the lead of Great Britain and outlaw handguns completely. The controversy here extends into what the Second Amendment really means.

At certain points, the Libertarian and the Liberal positions overlap; but at other points, they differ. Certainly, the strong enforcement of the equal protection clause of the Fourteenth Amendment has been a hallmark of the liberal position since the days in which FDR put minorities into coalition with the Democratic Party. Constitutional rights for women, for gays, for racial minorities and for seniors, receive more support from Liberals than they do from those on the other side of the aisle. Liberals are also apt to make more of First Amendment rights, as well as the Fourteenth Amendment. It hurts a liberal veteran just as much as some other kind of veteran to see an American flag burned, but the Liberal may tolerate it as the extreme expression of freedom of speech. Similarly, Liberals are more fearful of book censorship than are other groups. They tend to lend more support to the constitutional rights of students, teachers and professors.

On the abortion issue, Liberals tend to come down on the side of "choice" rather than "life." This is consistent with point ten in that it is one more illustration of their concern for women's rights. It is also consistent with their concern for over-population.

The final point is the liberal position on campaign finance. Liberals support restrictions on campaign funding, though they are bothered by the constitutionality of such proposals. History has a stern warning here. Two centuries before Christ, the great Roman Senate had degenerated into a place where seats could be bought, resulting in a struggle between the rich and the poor that literally tore that institution apart.

When Caesar brought his legions to support the rich, the Republic was history. When public office can be purchased, it is all over for representative democracy.

Some concluding observations are now needed. Do you have to hold all these positions to be a "Liberal"? Not unless you are an "illiberal" Liberal. Certainly, there are such. Can a Republican as well as a Democrat be a Liberal? Assuredly, they can be and have been. A large section of the eastern wing of the Republican Party probably qualifies as such. The label was actually used by a Republican Governor of New York and Vice President of the United States, the late Nelson Rockefeller. Admittedly, he was not well received by members of his own party here in the Midwest. It may be necessary to support more than one of these positions otherwise one could become a "single issue advocate" which does describe many in political life these days.

Above all we need tolerance now, as never before, for the other person's position. [Editorial Note: While observers may disagree as to whose fault it is, there can be little disagreement that, during the two terms of George W. Bush, ideological polarization has taken place.] Remember that, even though they could not agree on the time for lunch, Humphrey and Goldwater held each other in high respect when they stepped on the floor of the U.S. Senate. Remember also that, when Strom Thurmond was asked who he thought was the most competent U.S. Senator, he replied without blinking an eye, "Teddy Kennedy." Remember, finally, that Republics do not have long lives. Three or four centuries are about par for the course, and only the Athenian, Roman, English and American can qualify there. With a little more respect, tolerance and civility, we may set an historical record.

There are admitted problems with this "programmatic" definition of Liberalism. Hubert Humphrey, previously noted, pointed out the most obvious in that article. Each generation is confronted with its own issues and public policy questions. Therefore, it is necessary to re-write the definition of Liberalism every thirty years or so and that can be confusing. For a different approach to liberalism, one that seeks to find common threads that exist through out history, one should consult, *Liberalism: Time-tested Principle, for the Twenty-first Century*, a small volume by my colleague, Earl A. Reitan, Professor Emeritus of History at Illinois State University.

Finally, one must state what Liberalism is not. It is not Socialism. Occasionally, a credentialed Liberal will advocate the nationalization of something. John Kenneth Galbraith did that with the armaments industry in the United States. Few people saluted when he raised that flag on the pole. Nor is it Libertinism. Neo-conservatives have made great mileage for their cause in recent years by painting Liberals as in favor of gay marriages, unlimited abortion, atheism or at least agnosticism, pacifism, etc. Some Liberals may indeed be agnostics or pacifists, but those positions are not part of the major canon. The area of civil rights is complicated. Many Liberals support minority rights, including gay rights, and most Liberals are stalwart defenders of the first ten Amendments to the Constitution. While important to some, these positions are not necessarily in the main stream of the belief system. Nor is the separation of church and state, although that is important to many Liberals.

In our opinion, the heart of liberalism is economic, not social. It is the essential escape valve on the boiler of capitalism. Without that valve, a useful engine can explode and injure a lot of good people. It provides a safety net for those who are not high flyers in the capitalist system: the young, the elderly, the disabled, and the minorities. Without Liberalism, capitalism can degenerate into a jungle. Capitalists efficiently drive out the inefficient, all right, but who wants to live in that kind of a world? It is also the means by which we keep the inequalities produced by capitalism from tearing the Republic apart. Liberalism is not opposed to capitalism. Much to the contrary, it is the *sine quo non* of capitalism. An unregulated capitalism would cannibalize itself in a relatively short period of time.

Liberalism Revisited (Part I)

Santa Claus had nice gifts under the tree for citizens interested in political thought and public policy: two new books on Liberalism. Both are directed at finding the underlying principles of this approach to politics. The first is part of the continuing legacy of the late Paul Simon. It will come as no surprise that the Senator grounds his treatment of Liberalism in ethical principles. The man with the bow tie, the son of a Lutheran minister, was, after all, Mr. Clean, the very epitome of what an ethical statesman should be. The second book is the product of a Normal citizen who was for several decades a professor of British history at Illinois State University. The professor understandably traces the rise of Liberal principles in both British and American history. But Earl Reitan's book is no stale and stuffy erudite historical tome. Quite the contrary, the book applies these principles to the present Bush administration in a witty and entertaining way. In this two-part commentary, I will discuss both the Simon book, *Healing America*, and the Reitan book, *Liberalism: Time-tested Principles for the Twenty-first Century*. I will also add a few comments of my own on the subject of Liberalism

You could well argue that what the Senator has done is to write a small treatise on Christian Liberalism. But this is not the Christianity of the "born again" variety. This is a faith and a political belief centered on the notion of tolerance. In the Senator's own words, "It is strange but true that religion can be a factor for greater cruelty rather than for amelioration of a conflict. There are people in all camps who are spiritually deaf, who can only view any situation through the warped lens of extremists of their faith and never really listen to others. They are piling logs on the fires of violence" (p.27) From this principle, the Senator goes on to advocate greater foreign aid to the underprivileged of this world.

To support this position, the Senator points out that less than one-half of one percent of our federal budget goes to foreign aid and that we are now last among the 22 wealthy nations of the world in the percentage of our income that goes to helping the poor beyond our borders. This book is filled with facts and figures of this nature to buttress the many policy positions the Senator takes.

Much has been made of the fact that while the Senator was a committed Liberal, he was also a man who believed deeply in fiscal responsibility. Again, in his own words, "Put government on a pay-as-you-go basis. Where we want increased benefits, we must be willing to tax ourselves. If we are unwilling to tax ourselves, we should not get the services. Not following this policy weakens the economy and increases government's expenditures for interest, a regressive redistribution of wealth." (p.70) The Senator reminds us that President Truman paid for the Korean War with a tax increase but that, "We are being told that we need to increase defense expenditures by large amounts and that we should get tax cuts as a bonus. That may be great for me, but not for my grandchildren from whom we will be borrowing the money." (p.68) Again, "As of this writing, for fiscal year 2004, we will have a record-breaking deficit of $400 billion and a sizable tax cut. This may be good politics but it is bad economics." (P.56)

The Senator is also very much aware of the growing inequalities in the United States and the effect this has on politics. As he puts it: "The growing disparity between those who are more fortunate and those who are less fortunate is an invisible shift in our economy. It is not explosive now, nor will it be in the immediate future, but it will be explosive eventually if it is not addressed. The problem is worsening because, as a result of our system of campaign financing, those who are more fortunate play a disproportionate role in writing the tax laws." (p.125) The power of money in government troubles the Senator a great deal. He points out that the election of Michel Bloomberg for Mayor of New York cost more than the entire British nation spent on its last election.

Paul Simon's book is a call to action. As he says, "Professed noble values have no meaning unless people put legs on those ideas, unless citizens strive to make them a reality." (p.155) Readers will find that the book lays out a blue print for action on many public policy issues.

There are some minor imperfections in this book. For example, I would flunk the graduate student at Southern Illinois University who failed to check the Eugene Lang source and has Pericles giving a funeral tribute to Thucydides. (p.84) There are a number of redundancies in the book that a tougher editor would have caught. Nevertheless, this book was almost the Senator's deathbed testimony; it is a great one. In the next part of this commentary, I shall turn to Professor Reitan and to myself.

Liberalism Revisited (Part II)

In the first part of this commentary, I discussed the late Paul Simon's book, *Healing America*, and his approach to Liberalism. I turn now to the new book of Professor Emeritus Earl Reitan (Illinois State University) and his approach to the same subject. Professor Reitan traces the roots of Liberalism in the United States from the struggles between Alexander Hamilton and Thomas Jefferson, through the debates between the American Whigs and Andrew Jackson, to the turn of the century differences between the "Robber Barons" and the Progressives. Further, he pursues the subject through the era of the New Deal and finally into the conservative reaction to that era in Reaganism and the present Bush administration. It is a masterful job.

The Professor draws a careful distinction between Libertarians and Liberals. While the former have little use for a strong central government, the latter have much use for strong central government. The Liberals, he points out, use the Government as both a "ladder and a net." The ladder is to extend opportunities for all, largely through education, and the net is to make sure that none fall to the bottom in essential areas like health care, education, and minimum decent wages.

Professor Reitan has a precise view of what constitutes the political economy of Liberalism. In his words, "The essentials are clear enough: a strong federal government, abroad and at home; responsible federal finance, including a willingness to tax to meet national needs, a stable currency; and a substantial investment in our infrastructure, environment and people." (p.25) Like the late Senator Simon, Reitan takes a very dim view of fighting wars, "on the cuff." As he notes: "As in World War II, the President and Congress should expect to pay for the War (or a large part of it) through an increase in taxes. The notion that war can be waged without paying for it is an inducement to ill considered military action..... .The Vietnam War would probably not have been fought if the great American middle class had been called upon to pay for it through taxes and had not been given college deferments for its off-spring."(p.57)

In his book, Senator Simon had only a limited amount to say about foreign affairs. Reitan, by contrast, has a lot to say about foreign affairs. Not all of it will be accepted easily by his fellow Liberals. He feels that Liberals are often unrealistic in matters of foreign affairs. In his own words, "Liberals were true to American ideals when they declared the best way to extend democracy and freedom was to make the United States a shining example to the rest of the world.....Liberals lost their way, however, when they proclaimed their commitment to democracies in countries that totally lacked the pre-conditions of a liberal democratic government or society." (p.50) Reitan is clearly not much in favor of "nation building" and sees this as draining away much needed resources that could be better used at home.

Terrorism must be dealt with. At least, this particular Liberal is willing to concede the need for a strong military budget. However, Reitan sees this not in terms of a "war on terrorism," but rather in terms of a world wide police action against terrorists, in which we should have the support of many nations and of the United Nations, as well. Going it alone, in which we attempt to be policemen for the entire world, is not a viable option. It has led, he feels, to the misuse of the regular forces and an even greater misuse of the Reserves and the National Guard. I see one problem in viewing terrorism not as a war, but as a police action. What do you do when you really do have a "rogue nation"? True, Saddam, it turned out, did not posses the WMDs, but what do you do when some nation really does possess these weapons? A police action alone may simply not do the trick.

Between Reitan and Simon there is not much that is not covered, however, there are a two points that both did not address. Neither, for example, discusses the necessity of relieving state budgets through federal revenue sharing. Actions of the Bush administration in pushing down responsibilities to the state level and then not providing funds for those mandates is causing havoc with state budgets. An increased federal role in health care will help this situation, but it will not totally solve the problem. Federalism cannot function well without the resources to do the job. Illinois Senator Adlai Stevenson III introduced legislation of this nature, though it did not pass. It is time to look at that again.

Finally, while both men are extremely knowledgeable in both American and British history, neither seems to accept the notion that the "ship of state" just might sail better if we have periodic shifts between the liberal crew and the conservative crew. Historian, Arthur Schlesinger, Sr., formalized this idea into a theory. He believed that the pendulum swings back and forth between the liberal and the conservative positions at about a thirty-years time period. The pendulum, however, gets knocked out of sync by external forces like world wars and depressions. If this "self correcting" mechanism really does exist, it may do more for the salvation of this Republic, and of Western Civilization, than either Liberalism or Conservatism can do alone. One thing is certain. Simon and Reitan have elevated the political discourse far above the level that is currently heard on TV and radio. For that we should be profoundly grateful.

The Necessary Cost of Federalism

My conservative friends are constantly exalting the benefits of local control. This is usually in the context of "local control of education," but their case extends to all kinds of governments at the lower levels in a federal structure of governance. They are absolutely right on this issue. De Tocqueville, that shrewd observer of American government, makes a strong case for the importance of "lesser associations" in the defense of liberty. Federalism, it turns out, is almost as important as democracy itself.

However, on the Liberal side of the aisle, we keep pointing out a serious problem connected with decentralized governance and with local control that our conservative friends prefer to sweep under the rug. Unless resources, both human and material, are distributed relatively equally in geographic space, some of the state or local governments will have fine public services and others will have very poor levels of public service. This inequality, which often comes from over dependence on the property taxes, is most well known between school districts, but it also exists between police departments, fire departments, library boards and almost all other local services. It is a chronic problem associated with federalism. Like many chronic problems it is also treatable.

The treatment consists of grants-in-aid, which come from the superior level of government and go to the inferior level of government. They are intended to equalize the difference in resources between the inferior levels of government. We have them at the state level in state to local grants; we have them at the national level in national to state grants. So far, so good. Now comes the big problem. These state to local grants require higher state income taxes; the national to state grants require higher national income taxes. That very loud sound you just heard is my conservative friends falling right off the wagon. They constantly tell me, "There is no free lunch." They are dead right on that. But, they somehow forget, that federalism, while essential, comes with its own necessary costs.

Required National Service Bill

David Broder's recent column in the *Pantagraph* is on target. A required National Service Bill could now receive bi-partisan support. Long on the agenda of the Democratic side of aisle, it has recently picked up strength on the Republican side as well, notably from Senator McCain and the President. Unlike the old Universal Military Training bills, these new bills open the possibility of satisfying the two- or three-years requirement by other than military service, including the Peace Corps, AmeriCorps, and the President's new USA Freedom Corps. Presumably, all would be means of satisfying the requirement and neatly sidestep the conscientious objector problem. We might also solve some national security problems by including the Border Patrol and the Coast Guard. It also could be a solution to youth unemployment especially in urban and rural areas. If educational credits were attached to this kind of service, we also provide a way, similar to the GI Bill, of providing college and graduate school support to young men and women. It might even be extended to "faith based" organizations although here we run the risk of constitutional problems. Service in organizations like the Red Cross might pass the constitutional test.

Granted, it would require organizations like the old draft boards to administer fairly the new legislation, but these might be partially staffed on a volunteer basis and thus reduce administrative overhead. If something like this comes out of the terrorist problem, we will have found a silver lining in an otherwise very ugly cloud.

Random Thoughts on Galbraith and Schlesinger

[Editorial Note: Since this was written, *John Kenneth Galbraith, His Life, His Politics, His Economics* has appeared. Several tributes have also appeared, including an especially good one in *The Nation*, March 14, 2005.]

It is scary that Galbraith is 92 or 93 years old and Schlesinger is 82 or 83 years old. I cannot conceive of what the Liberal movement in America would be without both of these men. One an economist, more correctly a political economist, and the other an historian, they were definitely not "ivory tower" professors. Both served in the Roosevelt and Kennedy Administrations and consulted with Republican Administrations. They gave real meaning to that old saw, "How do you get into Government?" "You go to Harvard and turn left." History may record that Galbraith had the greater impact on American society because it fell to John Kenneth Galbraith to interpret to the American public the theory of another John, John Maynard Keynes. As they reach the end of their lives, surely all Liberals hope they receive the credit that is obviously due to them.

Both prolific writers, they must have turned out 35 or 40 books between them. Which of these had the greatest impact on the American public? For Galbraith I would argue that *The Affluent Society* and the *Culture of Contentment* are works of lasting importance in political economy. On the other hand, some smaller works like *The Scotch* and *Between Friends*, fill in the cracks to make Galbraith the humane being that he was. Galbraith has had, and will continue to have, his detractors. In the early days, a group on the Board of Overseers, the body that functions as a Board of Trustees for Harvard, tried to block the granting of tenure to Professor Galbraith on the grounds that he was too politically active for a

Harvard academic. The President of Harvard threatened to resign and the veto collapsed. Galbraith was elected President of the American Economic Association despite the fact that he took a dim view of turning all of economics into a branch of mathematics. For Ken, the world could not be reduced to a set of regression equations.

For Schlesinger, one certainly has to start with *The Age of Jackson*. Not only was this a Pulitzer Prize winner, but also it brought back into American history an interpretation based on class struggle, but one that was not Marxist. Schlesinger has been, and remains, the standard bearer of the NCL (non-communist left). Also widely read, more so than most history books, was *A Thousand Days: John F. Kennedy in the White House*. Schlesinger never neglected his historical duties as well. He reprised and extended his father's major theory on political swings in history in *The Cycles of American History*. More recently, he has started his autobiography, *A Life in the Twentieth Century*. It is devoutly hoped that he will have the strength to finish it.

About the best way to honor these men is to see that their books continue to be read and to be discussed. Therefore, I propose that the Stevenson Society establish a Galbraith/Schlesinger reading group. My wife and I will be glad to host such a group if we can get it up and running. There is no reason to limit our readings to Galbraith and Schlesinger in The New Liberal Canon, but that would be a darn good place to start.

Interpretation of the California Election

Everything is grist for the mill of ideologues, be they Conservative or Liberal. The conservative points to the nearly 60% Republican vote and claims, "We are a Reagan country again." The Liberal notes that the fiscal conservatism of Arnold Schwarzenegger is considerably moderated by his views on education and abortion. The younger Republicans reply that the actor is simply giving voice to the "softer and warmer" GOP of the elder Bush. This is all a lot of hogwash. The recent election in California said a lot about California, but not very much about national politics.

It is a shame that the Associated Press is not more generous with bylines. A recent unknown AP writer described California as "the spoiled American Dream." I wish I had written that. For the last decade or so, California has experienced a sluggish economy, considerable ethnic conflict, environmental problems, and a general exodus of people. The first thing a successful city dweller wants to do is buy a "ranch" or a "beach front" as far from the madding throng as he or she can and still get to work. Southern California's problem is people; too many people.

You don't need a graduate degree in sociology to know that population density causes major problems. But things are a lot worse when the zeitgeist is individualism. After all, when Horace Greeley said, "Go West, young man," he didn't mean to join a group. He meant to be your own boss and to do your own thing. That is darn hard to do when you are struggling just to find elbowroom. So, when your worldview and reality clash, then something or someone must be to blame. In that fine old American tradition of holding the establishment responsible, it had to be the Sacramento Democrats who were to blame because they have been dominant for the last ten years.

Arnold S. was elected without taking a position on any major public policy. The vote had nothing to do with politics. It had everything to do with Californian frustration.

George Half Right

George Will is assuredly not a half-wit. But, he is often just half right. In a recent *Pantagraph*, he made the perfectly valid point of saying that when the Democratic Party moves too far to the left, it gets beaten badly. He failed to tell you that when the Republican Party moves too far to the right, it also gets thrashed. Maybe he counts on no one's remembering the Goldwater debacle. Assuredly, no one will remember who Alf Landon was. That's not so bad. Will is a good conservative advocate; nothing requires him to make the liberal case.

However, when he slips into Liberal bashing—in this case, egghead bashing—he goes beyond the line. In Adlai Stevenson's hometown, Bloomington, Illinois, he will not get away with this. In the first place, trying to push conservatism into a populist mode just will not wash. Sure, there have been Conservatives who attempted to spring their party lose from their normal wealthy elite domination. The Lafollettes, Theodore Roosevelt, Wendell Wilkie, and Nelson Rockefeller come to mind. Do you remember what happened to them? They were over-whelmingly rejected by the rank and file of their party.

The truth is that there is a rather nasty strain of anti-intellectualism that runs in the conservative ranks. Most of the time, it is kept under control by the leadership; but, when it gets loose, it strikes both Liberals and Conservatives, alike. Thomas Dewey to a large extent was aban-doned by his own party, because he was thought to be too "intellectual." He was a fine Governor of New York and perhaps would have done just as well, if not better, than Harry Truman. Nelson Rockefeller was also considered "too smart" for his own party despite an excellent record, again, as governor of New York.

The problem is that Conservatives do not really believe in a meritocracy. They believe in an aristocracy; that often degenerates into a plutocracy. Well, I guess I must admit that Senator Fulbright hid his Phi Beta Kappa key under his overalls when he campaigned in Arkansas.

P. R. Plus

In a recent "Viewpoint" debate in the *Pantagraph*, former Illinois Representative Gerald Bradley has it right. We did "throw out the baby with the bath water" when we reduced the size of the Illinois House of Representatives and dropped proportional representation. However, we do not need to go back to the old system to correct the flaws of the present electoral method. Scotland shows us the way. In their new Parliament, the Scots combine single district with proportional representation, thus getting the benefits of both electoral systems. It is kind of like combining an analog system with a digital system.

One way it could work in Illinois would be to elect the current 118 Representatives just as they are now and then add 61 more Representatives elected by proportional representation. Yes, that would put us back at the levels of representation we had before we went to single districts, thereby increasing the public payroll. But, it should also end "safe districts" in which no minority party has a chance and in which the only real choice the voter has is in the primary ballot. We would need to create twenty large regional districts over the top of the 118 single unit districts. In these 20 regional districts, we would elect three representatives on the basis of the proportion of the vote received by each political party, adding one for a tiebreaker.

In many places, that would work out with Republicans entitled to two representatives and Democrats to the one remaining representative, or vice versa. In the second stage, the political parties would nominate the actual individuals and the voter would vote only for a party. The individuals to be elected would be published in order of priority (called "party lists" in Scotland). Rarely, would you need to go beyond the first or second individual ranked on a party's list.

All of this sounds much more complicated than it actually is. The system works to the advantage of the minority party, which in modern Scotland, happens to be the Conservative party. No finder's fee required. But, I "wooda refuse a wee dram if yo're a mind."

Nothing Wrong with the Ivins Plan

The book of Molly Ivins, who spoke recently at Illinois State University, was eighth on the national list of nonfiction best sellers as this was written. There must be more than just Liberals reading *Bushwhacked*. However, in the event some frugal Conservatives do not want to cough up the twenty-seven bucks to buy their own copy, here are some points from her final chapter that need discussion.

First, push campaign financing reform and get us out of the "cash and carry" status we are in now. That is, you bring in the cash and carry out what legislation you want. She cites the Arizona system as a model. Second, end the enormous Gerrymandering of congressional districts in most states. California has reached a point where there may be only one really swing district in the entire state, the rest are "safe seats." She cites Iowa as a possible model.

On the economic side, she allows that the economy can be jump-started by either tax cutting or pump priming, but tax cuts to the wealthy and expenditures through the military will not do it. Try tax cuts to the lower- and middle-income groups and spending on infra-structure and education. The American Society of Civil Engineers claims we have two trillion dollars in neglected physical infrastructure needs, alone. Do you really wonder about blackouts in major American cities with that unmet-need staring you in the face?

Here is one she does not mention. How long can we continue a policy of spend and borrow before our currency starts sliding relative to the rest of the world? Have you looked at the ratio of the Euro to the dollar recently? Sure, a cheaper dollar might just bring more tourists to the USA from Europe. Well now, do you really think any European wants to visit a county that has systematically backed away from many of its treaty obligations and has announced to the world that it will "go it alone"? What fool would want to be in the United States when some other nation launches its own "preventive strike"?

Democrats Need to Return to Their Roots

As Dr. Dean takes over the reins of the Democratic Party, strong consideration should be given to returning to the historical stance of that party. This is the party of Thomas Jefferson who opposed the Federalists. This is the party of Andrew Jackson who opposed the National Republicans and then the Whigs. This is the party of William Jennings Bryan who opposed the Republicans. This is even the party of Teddy Roosevelt, whose Progressive Party out-polled the Republicans in 1912. Of course, it is also the party of FDR, JFK, and Lyndon Johnson.

What do they all have in common? Every one of them opposed an aristocracy of wealth, a plutocracy, which they believed a threat to the Republic. At earlier points in our history, we had to rely on anecdotal evidence of growing concentrations of income and wealth. Now, hard data are available to show the growing concentration of wealth in the last decade of the 19th Century and the first decade of the 20th Century. Growing inequalities in both wealth and income are evident in the last two decades of the 20th Century. Both the Democratic Party and Progressive Republicans stood resolutely against these growing inequalities.

From the days when the Federalists claimed that Jefferson intended to bring the French Revolution to the shores of the United States to the present moment, the party of wealth and privilege has always accused the more popular party of provoking "class warfare." That has always been a red herring (pun intended). The purpose of the more popular party has consistently been to build up a large middle class of home-owning, relatively well-educated citizens. This stable, informed middle class would then act as a buffer between the very rich and the very poor, thus preventing class warfare, rather than bringing it on. The Democrats want the "ownership society," but they should resist, with every ounce of strength they have, the ownership by the one percent of the other ninety-nine percent. Neither capitalism nor the Republic can survive when capital is over concentrated.

The Pendulum

In the tradition of De Tocqueville and Crevecour, two Brits, John Micklethwait and Adrian Woolridge, have produced a well-documented and well-written book entitled, *The Right Nation: Conservative Power in America*. One of the conclusions of that book is: "Liberalism as a governing philosophy is dead." Don't believe it. If you can lift yourself above the din of partisan battle, a pattern will emerge.

Historians, not the least of them the Schlesingers, father and son, write of swings in the pendulum down through time from Conservative to Liberal poles. Political Scientists tend to speak of "major realignments" in political parties through time. These appear to occur about once in a generation; say once in every 30 to 40 years. If the average person lives long enough, he or she will see at least one of these reconfigurations and sometimes a second one.

There have been two of these realignments in the last century. Franklin Roosevelt put together the Democratic coalition that brought about the New Deal. That was then extended and solidified by the Great Society of John Kennedy and Lyndon Johnson. In 1980, Ronald Reagan pulled together elements of a Republican coalition that Richard Nixon had first begun to assemble. Previous to that, a powerful group headed by large business and banking interests, forged a coalition during the McKinley administration that would last, despite Teddy Roosevelt, all the way from 1890 to 1932.

Unfortunately, cleometrics is not an exact science. These swings tend to be jarred out of shape by wars and other external pressures. Therefore, it is difficult to say when one swing ends and another starts. My own interpretation of things at present is that the conservative wave that started rolling in around 1980 is now moving toward its crest. An ebb tide will come, but perhaps not until around 2012. So take heart, Liberals, your time at bat will come again.

The swings of this pendulum are natural and normal. Indeed, they constitute the pulse of a healthy democracy. The time for concern is when you cannot hear the pendulum swinging.

Borrow and Spend

"Our Views" in the March 27th *Pantagraph* was right on the point. However, Governor Blagojevich, who is your candidate for the president of the "Borrow and Spend Club," is just out of luck. Another president already holds that job—the man from Crawford, Texas, who learned the part well from yet another president, Ronald Reagan. You remember Ronald. He is the one of whom our Vice President said, "Reagan taught us that deficits don't really matter."

So, don't worry about the cost of that Iraq war, just put that cost in your grandchildren's Christmas stocking. Short money for social security payments? Just steal it from the "surplus" in the social security trust. When it comes time to use that same "surplus" for future retirees, stick your grandchildren with that bill, as well. Those badly needed drugs for grandmother and granddad? Just put that on the little toddler's tab, too. Is tax and spend beginning to look pretty good to you? Thought it would.

Oh, yes, and remember that gut busting school finance problem you have in most of the states? Well, when "W" gave those tax reductions to the rich, he simultaneously cut the yield on your state income tax. You see, in most states, your state tax liability is based on your federal income tax liability. So, when, for lack of state funds, your grandchild goes to an impoverished school, he or she will not get a good enough education to pay all those other bills you just shoved down their little throats. "Wave at that pretty Cadillac going down the road, little darling, that's where a part of your school money went."

Now, that loud cry you hear off stage? No, it's not the voice of Hamlet's ghost. It's the pitiful sound of the old Republican Party. You remember that outfit that once was known to be fiscally responsible. (To be truthful, it really was, a long time ago.)

Section II

"You can have great inequalities of wealth or you can have a democracy. You cannot have both."

—Mr. Justice Brandeis

II. Inequalities in Income and Wealth

A. Do the Democrats Advocate Class Warfare?

B. Sir Karl Popper, Class Warfare, and Today's World

C. Meritocracy, Yes; Aristocracy, No

D. Government Benefits: Who Will Pay?

E. The Fading American Dream

F. Qualified Students Denied Admission

G. Fairness in Compensation

H. Time for Teddy, Again

Do the Democrats Advocate Class Warfare?

President Bush constantly attempts to parry criticism of his tax cuts for the wealthy by accusing his Democratic critics of advocating "Class warfare." George W. may not actually know what the term means. If he understands it to mean what it means in Marxist literature (the violent overthrow of the government by the representatives of the working class), then he is sadly off base. No responsible Democrat has ever advocated the "Dictatorship of the Proletariat." None ever will. Even Lenin could not get all Marxists to subscribe to his view of overthrowing duly elected governments by force of arms. The Dictatorship was mostly Lenin's own contribution to Marxist thought. It was not the primary emphasis of Karl Marx.

Harking back all the way to Aristotle, many Democrats believe that a society is most stable if it consists of a large middle class with smaller rich and poor classes. "Class warfare" occurs when the middle class disappears, or was never there in the first place, and the society then breaks into two warring segments, the very rich and the very poor. Thus the classic 19th Century liberal position in Europe was in support of the bourgeoisie (the merchant class) and in opposition to the landed gentry. They were also in opposition to the uneducated mob. It may be a serious and a fair criticism of the modern Democratic Party in the United States that they have not done enough for middle-income people. If so, then Republican initiatives directed specifically toward that middle-income group, and not, as they are now, toward the upper-income group, should be richly rewarded at the polls.

If what the President really means is "class struggle" rather than "class warfare," he may be closer to the truth. A long line of Democratic Presidents has laid the basis for this. Jefferson opposed the landed gentry in the United States even though he himself came from the gentry. Early in Jefferson's career, he observed the landed gentry in England and France and cared little for what he saw, especially in England. General Andrew Jackson astounded the conservative Whigs when he tracked the muddy boots of his frontiersmen through the White House. Franklin D. Roosevelt put together the coalition of overlooked and forgotten minorities that is still an important part of the Democratic Party. Truman continued that with his civil rights legislation. Johnson said he specifically came to perfect the New Deal. And finally, JFK's "shining city on the hill," his Camelot, was intended to be the establishment of the meritocracy, a government of the best. This was to be preferred over the plutocracy, a government of the rich. Now, if THAT is what "W" objects to, then he has the Democrats dead to rights. From Thomas Jefferson to the present time, the oldest political party in this nation has indeed engaged in class struggle for the less fortunate. Many of us would not have it any other way.

Bloomington's favorite son, Adlai Stevenson, was asked once if he was a Socialist. Adlai replied, "No sir, I'm just a garden variety Democrat." Will Rogers once remarked, "I am a member of no ORGANIZED political party. I am a Democrat." We deliberately set a big tent on both sides of the aisle in this country. It may become a little uncomfortable for Conservatives in the Democratic tent, and it may become a little uncomfortable for Liberals in the Republican tent, but they are seldom driven into the desert by their colleagues with the biblical injunction, "Now look to your own tent, David." This pull toward the center, this desire for consensus, and this need for compromise may be the essence of good democratic governance. Presidents from both parties, including the one now in office, are badly advised if they insist on ideological purity at the expense of pragmatic solutions to problems of public policy. Franklin Delano Roosevelt could have chosen a strict socialist ideology when confronted by the great depression. He was certainly urged to do so by many, but he did not. He chose pragmatism. He chose whatever worked. But then, FDR, a Harvard graduate, didn't squeak through Yale by electing pass-fail options on all the courses in his senior year, did he?

Sir Karl Popper, Class Warfare, and Today's World

A half of a century ago, while attending Wabash College, I was assigned a chapter in what was then a relatively new book. It was the final chapter of volume one of Karl Raimund Popper's *The Open Society and Its Enemies*. My computer collapsed recently, hence the opportunity to go back and not only re-read that chapter, but read the entire work. No, I am not going to subject anyone to a book review of a half-century-old study in political philosophy. But there are some ideas concerning "class warfare" that are still pertinent to today's world.

Professor Popper fled his native Austria in 1938, when Hitler proclaimed the "Anschluss" and occupied that country. Popper ended up in New Zealand for the duration of World War II, teaching in a relatively low-paying position in a small college. During his enforced exile, he began to systematically explore the roots of the totalitarian philosophy that had sent him scurrying half way around the world. In particular, he looked to the writings of Plato, Hegel, and Marx to see if he could find there the seeds of totalitarianism.

He found what he was looking for and a great deal more. Both Plato and Aristotle agreed that a major cause of the social unrest in the Greek City States was the continual warfare between the rich and the poor. But their response to "class war" was quite different. Plato sought stability and security in a state governed by a philosopher king, or if that could not be done, then by "Guardians" who were especially trained for the task. "The wise should rule and the ignorant should be ruled," concluded Plato, in one of the earliest known statements of meritocracy that can be found. Note Plato did not say, "The rich should rule and the poor should be ruled." (Plutocracy) In fact, Plato's "Guardians" were absolutely forbidden from engaging in any business or industry whatsoever. Popper argues that Plato might have meant, "The learned shall rule and the stupid shall be ruled." (Sophocracy) As a former professor, I can tell you that form of government would surely be a disaster.

Aristotle also sought the "government of the best." However, in the Third Book of the *Politics*, Aristotle described equilibrium of social classes, which, although not the "best state," could be a very stable state. Said Aristotle: If a society can be composed of a small poor class and also a small rich class, then it would also necessarily have a large middle class. That kind of society, the Sage observed, can exist for a very long time. In over two millennia, we have not been able to improve on that political and economic observation. True, although today's political economists tend to speak more of the dangers of an "over concentration of wealth" rather than of an "unequal distribution of wealth," the concepts are related. Both Plato and Aristotle concluded that "class warfare," though always just over the horizon, need not necessarily lead to the collapse of the state.

Karl Marx, also an exile from a war-torn Europe and writing in the midst of Victorian hard times, came to quite a different conclusion. Like Plato and like Aristotle, he thought that the instability of any society was basically derived from the continuing conflict between the rich and the poor. But, unlike Plato and Aristotle, he did not think this warfare could be avoided. In fact, he found the struggle between the rich and the poor to be the central theme in all history. Marx did not necessarily believe, however, that this warfare must always and in all cases, pass through a dictatorship of the poor (the Proletariat). Later in his life, Marx specifically stated that a violent revolution might not be necessary in Great Britain and in America.

How does all this relate to us today? Both conservative and liberal economists now agree that the last thirty years in the United States have seen a striking decrease in the size of the middle class. As a special article in the *Washington Post* (Sept. 27, 2004) points out, the number of families over $75,000 a year has increased greatly and the number under $35,000 has also increased in the last three decades. However, in the middle section, there has been a decrease. It is doubtful that anyone would argue that this is the "impoverishment of the middle class" long predicted by Karl Marx; nevertheless, it is a worrisome trend. No less than Alan Greenspan, not exactly a rampant Liberal, has said this is a development that is not at all favorable to the Republic.

Sir Karl concluded his masterwork on much the same note as Lord Acton. Acton believed that the long struggle to establish liberty was the main moving force in all history. Popper believed there was no "meaning" to history, but that we could "give it meaning." One meaning History might have would be to show us how to control political power. Sir Karl Popper died in 1994, having lived long enough to see the triumph of his "open society" throughout much of the world.

There are at least two questions left open in Popper's treatment of the open society and its enemies. Can the open society survive an onslaught by the "true believer," usually of some religious belief? Popper handled Arnold Toynbee with kid gloves on this very issue. Of course, it is not possible to know how he would have felt about the clash of civilizations thesis advanced by Samuel P. Huntington. Popper's world is that of rationalism. What happens to that world when it is confronted with massive attacks by suicide martyrs, equipped with suitcase-size atomic devices, is not at all clear. Also, Popper's rationalism caused him to question the practicality of Woodrow Wilson's attempt to extend Democracy to the entire world. Likely he would now question George W. Bush's attempt to do the same thing in the Middle East. Popper was the quintessential pragmatist. Don't try for the master solution and don't look for the authoritative answer, just solve the problems one at a time, and make sure your back is covered. Somehow, I suspect Henry Kissinger had a copy of *The Open Society and Its Enemies* on his bookshelf.

Meritocracy, Yes;
Aristocracy, No

The recent awarding of a Knighthood of the British Empire to Alan Greenspan is certainly appropriate and constitutes the best use of the Queen's honors list. The British have been careful about this. Much improvement has taken place from the time when a Knighthood could be purchased by a large enough contribution to the Conservative and Unionist Party. We, Americans, lack the equivalent for awarding our own meritorious people; we are much the poorer for it. Sadly, we seem intent on awarding the accumulation of wealth, rather than the accumulation of merit. Thomas Jefferson must be rolling in his grave.

Jefferson and like-minded Founding Fathers were fearful of the establishment of a landed aristocracy in this country. For that reason, they prohibited the practices of primogeniture and entail in the United States. That is, land cannot be passed only to the oldest male heir and the heirs cannot be prevented from selling the land. The creation of Trusts has gotten around some of these restrictions, but not completely. Most countries also prevent land from being passed from one generation to another without paying a price for that privilege. We had such a tax until the Reagan and Bush Administrations launched a successful campaign to repeal the inheritance tax. At present, up to two-thirds of a million dollars in wealth or in land or in anything else can be passed to children without federal tax. The "neo-coms" predict that this kind of tax eventually will be entirely eliminated in the United States. Few countries in this world are so generous to their wealthy citizens.

The rationale behind the elimination of the inheritance tax in this country is that a father and mother had some sort of "right," not a "privilege," to pass on their money to their children, if that was their wish. Within limits, that does not seem unreasonable. But is it reasonable to be able to pass on millions of dollars, which the father and mother, themselves, probably did not earn, to their children, who certainly did not merit, by any action of their own, these large rewards? I think not. When you couple this action with the lowering of the income tax, especially in the upper brackets, and with the lowering of the capital gains tax, the stage is set for the creation of an aristocracy in this nation. This new aristocracy is not based on land alone, but on all forms of wealth. Of course, if the stock market continues its slide, we will not have to worry about any adverse effects of lowering the capital gains tax since there will be bloody few capital gains for anybody.

It must also be admitted that aristocracies are not all bad. A good case can be made that without aristocracies there would be fewer fine arts in this world. Historically, aristocracies have been good patrons of the arts and have supported scholars and universities well. History does not fully record what surrender of independence that caused. Regrettably, as Aristotle pointed out over two millennia ago, "government by the best" tends over time to degenerate into "government by the powerful." Therefore, we must constantly guard against the rise of an Oligarchy in the United States. We have not been doing a very good job of this recently.

Jefferson was so fearful of the inheritance of both wealth and honors that he opposed the establishment of the Order of Cincinnatus. That Order, that still exists today, was intended for men and women who could trace their ancestry to an Officer in the Revolutionary Army. However, Jefferson believed strongly in the establishment of a Meritocracy. He made that absolutely clear in his letters to John Adams. He also made it clear that he regarded the establishment of the University of Virginia as an equal achievement to the writing of the Declaration of Independence. We forget, at our considerable peril, what the Sage of Monticello taught us

Government Benefits: Who Will Pay?

In "Your Views" in a recent *Pantagraph*, Philip Buffington draws the conclusion that the social and educational investments proposed by Senator Kerry will come from taxation of the middle class. He argues that this will be true because, "the great wealth of this country is held by the middle class." I certainly wish this were the case. It is not true now and never has been in recent years.

At the end of the "roaring twenties," about half of aggregate net worth in the USA was held by the richest one percent of households. This gradually declined until 1980, when somewhat more than twenty percent of aggregate net worth was held by the very rich. Starting with the election of Ronald Reagan, this figure started back up again until at present it is just short of forty percent of aggregate net worth.

Comparisons with Great Britain are revealing. From the 1920s till the 1960s, wealth inequalities were greater in the UK than in the USA. I assume many remember the world of "Up Stairs; Down Stairs." From 1960 until 1980, they were about equal. However, from 1980s to the present, wealth inequalities are greater in the USA than in the UK. In fact, our wealth inequalities are now greater than in any developed country in the world.

Sorry, Mr. Buffington, the middle class cannot pay for the Kerry proposals; they just do not have the money. Try the rich.

[Editorial Note: For an excellent analysis on how much the Bush tax cuts have aggravated this matter, see: David C. Johnston, "Richest Are Leaving Even the Rich Far Behind," *New York Times*, June 5, 2005.]

The Fading American Dream

Several recent books (K. Phillips, *Wealth and Democracy*; W.G. Gates, Sr, *Wealth and Our Commonwealth*; E.D. Wolff; *Top Heavy*; G. Hodgson, *More Equal Than Others*) have documented the fact that, in the last three decades of the 20th Century, both wealth and income have become much more concentrated in this country. There are fewer households in the middle range, more in the poorer range, and a lot more in the higher income range. We know that this has happened at least twice before in this country: once in the 1890's (the Gilded Age) and once in the 1920's (the Roaring Twenties). Ominously, both times, an increase in the concentration of wealth and income was followed by a severe depression.

So what? Is this not the price one must pay for having a private enterprise system? Some win, but some must lose. Perhaps, especially since developing countries like India and China are now starting to experiment with the free market system and are showing this tendency toward wealth concentration. If this is so, we must be aware of the high price we are paying. The rich have good schools; the poor have lousy schools. The income inequality also warps the market into an hourglass. Luxury goods and services are for the upper part of the hourglass and K-Mart for the lower part. Falling demand in the middle class slides the economy into recession or depression. Even the military is affected. An officer class may remain, but the quality level of the non-coms and the common soldier declines.

Some Conservatives believe that, as long as there is strong upward mobility between income levels, this is not a serious problem. This is a valid point. However, a study conducted by the Federal Reserve Bank of Boston and published by *Business Week* shows that upward mobility was much greater in the 1970s than in the 1980s in this country. Further, another study by the Century Foundation shows that upward mobility is now greater in Finland, Sweden, Canada, and Germany than it is in the USA. A full review of the most recent mobility studies by David Wessel can be found in *The Wall Street Journal* of May 13, 2005. Mr. Wessel concludes that the weight of the evidence shows that upward social mobility has lessened in the last quarter of a century in the United States. Regrettably, the "American Dream" of rags to riches may be fading. It is becoming riches to riches and rags to rags.

So what can we do? Well, what we should certainly NOT do is to follow the policy recommendations of the Bush Administration. Tax cuts for the rich can only make the disparity in income and wealth worse than it now is. Also, the repeal of the federal inheritance (estate) tax will simply make it easier for the wealthy to pass their large incomes, earned in the last three decades, into the 21st Century. Admittedly, there needs to be a high exemption on this tax, so that the inheritances of family farms and small businesses are not jeopardized. Much inherited wealth, of course, totally escapes any tax through the use of family trusts. Ultimately, if these trends continue, we may have to consider the taxation of wealth, in addition to the taxation of income, such as is done in Switzerland, Denmark, Netherlands and ten other European nations.

Can education be a help?* Yes, both common sense and detailed economic studies (Arrow, *Meritocracy*) prove that education is a strong factor in upward mobility. Apparently, President Summers at Harvard believes this. Beginning this fall, if students are admitted and if they come from families with less than $43,000 annual income, they can receive a free ride at Harvard College—no tuition, no fees, zip. Other high profile universities may follow this example. But this will not help the many who are educated in state colleges and universities, such as Illinois State University. There, the lack of state money will not allow such largesse. Can the government do something? Yes, Senator Kerry has a plan to give two years of college free to those who would give two years of service to the government, a sort of mini GI Bill. The Senator has also pledged to increase the Pell Grants, which go to low-income students trying to attend colleges and universities.

Some will say this is merely playing the "class warfare card" in American politics. Much to the contrary, this is an attempt to save the middle class from extinction, thus avoiding class warfare. Over two millennia ago, Aristotle told us that the middle class was essential to the continued existence of any body politic. History also tells us that the over concentration of wealth was a prime factor in the fall of many previous republics, Rome, Renaissance Italy, the Dutch Republic, and that this same over concentration corrupted many British attempts at representative governance. Among American Presidents who have warned us of the danger of over concentration of wealth and income to this Republic, we find Thomas Jefferson, Andrew Jackson, Abraham Lincoln, Theodore Roosevelt, Woodrow Wilson, Franklin Roosevelt, Dwight Eisenhower and Richard Nixon. If these are the soldiers of class warfare, then show me the enlistment papers.

*[Editorial Note: For a view that education is not a solution, but rather part of the problem, see: David Brooks, "Karl's New Manifesto," *New York Times*, May 29, 2005.]

Qualified Students Denied Admission

[Editorial Note: As an editorial in the *New York Times*, June 7, 2005, notes: much of the problem of denied access to higher education is caused by underfunding Pell Grants and providing smaller veterans' educational benefits than was the case in the past.]

Illinois State University has reached the point where budget cuts are causing qualified students to be denied admission. This is clearly wrong. Thomas Jefferson, De Tocqueville, and Lord Acton, among others, clearly saw that wide access to higher education was one of the most important matters that differentiated this Republic from the status-bound societies of old Europe. Carried far enough, this situation becomes a major danger to any democratic society. What can be done about it? First, the faculty can be asked to assume larger class sizes, but this has its limitations. Undergraduate classes are already too large at ISU and increasing graduate class sizes dilutes the graduate experience. Secondly, the administration at ISU can be encouraged to take an even more rigorous stance relative to these cuts. President Boschini took some bold positions, but even more intestinal fortitude is now required.

Every time a qualified student is rejected, the letter denying admission should clearly state that the reason for this denial was not lack of qualifications, but lack of space due to budget cuts. Further, at regular intervals, the University President should deliver these letters to Senator Brady, with the request that they be read into the record from the floor of the Senate. The Senator should not be asked to come up with budget solutions at these times. However, the public needs to know every time a qualified student has been denied admission to this public university. Remember that the General Assembly rarely initiates a solution to a problem. The General Assembly reacts to problems that the public presents to it.

Do not be turned aside here by those who say that nothing can be done due to the state's poor financial situation. In the first place, our income tax rates are still low relative to those in surrounding states. It is true that the yields from any income tax will fall as income falls. But the per capita income in Illinois has not declined that much. If the argument is that we are now denying qualified students admission because we are in a major recession, then let the Governor have the guts to say exactly that.

Fairness in Compensation

To be sure, the world of private enterprise does not attach much weight to the concept of "fairness." However, some facts are so egregiously wrong that they must be brought to the public's attention. Owners and entrepreneurs are surely entitled to a fair profit on their capital and their management skills. But what constitutes a "fair" profit?

Suppose we offer as a criterion of fairness that the percentage of increase in total compensation in salaries and wages should be roughly equal to the percentage of increase in corporate profits, after taxes. If we look at those two percentages over the last forty years, they do look quite similar. 7.6 percent for salaries and wages and 7.2 percent for after tax corporate profits. A ratio any union would probably accept as "fair." However, following that sequence through time yields some disturbing results. For the last ten years, the percentage increases are 5.2 percent in total wage compensation as contrasted with 7.6 percent in after tax corporate profits. For the last five years, it is 4.1 percent in wages as compared to 6.2 percent in corporate profits. Perhaps still not greatly out of line given the amount of risk assumed in the corporate sector these days.

However, the last three years show a wage increase of only 1.3 percent and a corporate profit increase of 14.4 percent. That is surely out of line. If these profits had been passed along to share holders, that might offer some mitigating circumstances; but, much of these profits have been consumed by increasing CEO salaries that are far out of line with other countries. What to do? Well, support your local unions. If that does not work, call the attention of your Senator and Congressman to this unfair situation. The "hidden hand" of capitalist mythology does not seem to be working very well in the labor market these days. Perhaps it needs some assistance from government.

[Note: I am indebted to a Google researcher for calculating these percentages at my request.]

Time for Teddy, Again

As we reflect on the lessons of the last election, we might do well to recall the man who said: "By the time I became President I had grown to feel with deep intensity of conviction that governmental agencies must find their justification largely in the way in which they are used for the practical betterment of living and working conditions among the mass of the people." Franklin Roosevelt, you say, or JFK, or Lyndon Johnson? Wrong. He was a Republican, at least until the bankers, the corporate interests, and the oligarchy of wealth drove Theodore Roosevelt to found his own political party, the Progressive Party. It should be well remembered that, in 1912, the Progressive party outvoted the regular Republican Party in this nation.

"Teddy" believed in the "Square Deal." As he said, "I shall uphold justice whether the man accused of guilt has behind him the wealthiest corporations, the greatest aggregations of riches in this country, or whether he has behind him the most influential labor organizations in the country." He also called for a sea change in economic thinking: "…we must abandon definitely the *laissez-faire* theory of political economy and fearlessly champion a system of increased Governmental control…. As has been aptly said, the only way to meet a billion dollar corporation is with a one hundred billion dollar government."

"T.R." was a religious man; but, in his book on Oliver Cromwell, he gave this warning, "It is very essential that a man should have in him the capacity to defy his fellows if he thinks that they are doing the work of the devil and not the work of the Lord. It is even more essential, however, that he be most cautious about mistaking his own views for that of the Lord."

If "T.R." were still with us, he would most strongly support the views of former Secretary of Labor, Robert B. Reich. Said Reich: "Democrats used to speak passionately about social justice and it should still be the core of the Democrats' morality." He went on to say that it is, "morally wrong to give huge tax cuts to the rich while cutting social programs for the poor and working class, especially when the gap between the rich and the poor is greater than it has been for an entire century in this country."

Without doubt, the Bush II Administration is the most wealth-friendly administration we have had since the McKinley Administration at the end of the 19th Century. It is instructive to look at what former Presidents have said about the effect of wealth on this Republic. We start, of course, with Jefferson: "I hope we shall crush in its birth the aristocracy of our moneyed corporations, which dare already to challenge our government to a trial of strength and bid defiance to the laws of our country." Then, to Lincoln: "I see in the near future a crisis approaching that unnerves me and causes me to tremble for the safety of my country. As a result of the war, corporations have been enthroned and an era of corruption in high places will follow, and the money power of the country will endeavor to prolong its reign by working on the prejudices of the people until all wealth is aggregated in a few hands and the Republic is destroyed." Back to "T.R.," we find: "Of all forms of tyranny the least attractive and the most vulgar is the tyranny of mere wealth." And, from his cousin, Franklin D.: "The real truth of the matter is, as you and I know, that a financial element in the large centers has owned the government of the United States since the days of Andrew Jackson."

If Presidents are not enough, then how about bankers? J.P. Morgan repeated "T.R.'s" words and added the phrase, "the tyranny of plutocracy." Ramsey Clark completed that thought by saying: "We are not a Democracy. It is a terrible misunderstanding and a slander to call us that. In reality, we are a plutocracy, a government of the wealthy." Judges and lawyers generally have the last word, so to Mr. Justice Brandeis, who, paraphrasing Aristotle, said: "You can have great inequalities of wealth or you can have a democracy. You cannot have both."

The time has come again for us to look at the progressive principles of Teddy Roosevelt. We do not need to found a third party to do that, however. We can work within both the Democratic and Republican Parties to see that economic populism finds it voice again. It may, admittedly, be more difficult now within the present Republican Party, because the progressive spirit has been allowed to die there. A new coalition of Progressives, Liberals, and Independents is needed to steer the ship of state away from the rocks and shoals of concentrated wealth.

Section III

"Taxation is the price of Civilization."

—Justice Oliver Wendell Homes

"Don't ask for these services unless you are ready to pay for them."

—Senator Paul Simon

III. School Finance and Related Public Policy

A. Education As a Civil Right

B. School Funding for Democrats and Progressive Republicans

C. Taxation, Politics and Education

D. Taxation Reform: Key to Education Funding Crisis

E. Is Ricardo Still Right?

F. The Federal Role in Education

G. School Vouchers: Solution or Another Problem

H. A Mistake Corrected: A Note on Cost Effectiveness

I. Unit Five School Board Shows Guts

J. Privatization of Education: A Mistake

K. Governor's Cure Worse Than the Disease

L. House Bill 750

M. Outline of Prospective Legislation for an Annual Equity Report

N. Significant Dates in Illinois School Finance

Education As a Civil Right

In the a recent edition of the *Pantagraph*, Marsha Mercer posses the question, "Is reading a civil right for every American?" She then explains that President Bush has been answering that question in the affirmative for the last couple of years. We have a long history with that question in Illinois. We frame it differently, asking rather, "Is education a fundamental constitutional right?" But, before I recite some of that state's history, it may be useful to view this question at the federal level.

The word "education" appears nowhere in the federal constitution. It is true that there are a few lawyers and scholars who believe that it might be possible to extrapolate a fundamental right to education from the First Amendment or perhaps the Fifth Amendment. However, that group is very small and includes almost none of the advisors of George W. Bush, who tend to be, as Mercer points out, strict constructionists. Most lawyers and scholars believe that for education to become a fundamental constitutional right, it would be necessary to amend the federal constitution. That is not unthinkable, but it requires organizations ready to carry the process through the Congress and then through the requisite number of states. Individuals in some of the national educational organizations have said they are willing to do that, but is George W. Bush now prepared to lead that national effort?

If he does, he will join that small group of Republicans who believe in the concept of "education as a unique public function." That was an idea put forward many decades ago by Professor Judd of the University of Chicago. The idea was that education was not like other governmental services. The return to the public from an investment in education was believed to be much larger than the return from investing in other public services. This idea foreshadowed the "human capital" school of thought in Economics. The principle advocate of this position on the national scene was "Mr. Republican," the late Senator Robert Taft of Ohio. In Illinois, our own state senator, John Maitland, often expressed the same notion. Skeptics, however, are not going to place much credence in President Bush's position.

Let us turn to the relevant record in Illinois. In the early 1990s, a group of professors at Illinois State University reviewed the constitutional challenges to school finance systems that had then been going forward in other states for twenty years and decided that Illinois should launch a constitutional challenge to our system of funding the K-12 schools. They invited to Normal every district superintendent they thought would support that legal challenge. On the eve of the meeting, there was a blizzard that knocked out all of the electricity on the campus except the power in University High School. I walked over to U High expecting absolutely no one to be there. When I opened the door, I found that the auditorium was packed. I remember turning to my colleague, Ben Hubbard, and saying, "If they come through a blizzard for this, then the die is cast." He nodded and said, "Yes, now we must go forward with it." So, the case was launched with the help of many good men and women. With the considerable help of a local attorney, Robert J. Lenz, an organization was put together to fight the cause. Funds to support the litigation were obtained from the Joyce Foundation and from many school districts. The state moved to dismiss; won at the district court level; was sustained at the appeals level; and won decisively, five to one with one judge abstaining, at the Supreme Court level. The decision in the *Committee v. Edgar* states clearly that in Illinois education is NOT a constitutional right. To be sure, it is a fundamental constitutional right in almost half of the other states, including President Bush's Texas, but NOT in Illinois. That is the law in Illinois to this day.

Before the decision was announced, a different group of professors at Illinois State University met with legislators, including Senator John Maitland and Senator Art Berman. This group decided to carry an amendment to the Illinois Constitution that would change the wording of Article Ten (the Education Article) so that the state's constitution would then clearly proclaim that education was a fundamental right. The amendment was based largely on the work of Professor David Franklin, then a member of the Illinois State University faculty, who had studied education articles in all fifty states. During the campaign to pass the amendment, Senator John Maitland made over 50 speeches advocating passage. I made over 30. I recall one meeting in the offices of the *Pantagraph* where an irate Senator Maitland shouted at the then publisher, because this paper refused to support the amendment. We needed a super majority; we failed by only a few percentage points, surpassing the Presidential candidate and the candidate for the Unite States Senate at that election. The failure of passage may be laid at the feet of several business groups that strongly opposed the measure and directly at the feet of Governor Jim Edgar, who belatedly came out against the amendment. The failure of the court case and the failure of the amendment shortened several academic careers, including mine. Looking back on those events though, I think I can agree with General Longstreet. Longstreet said, after the battle of Gettysburg, "To lose a battle that important, a lot of men had to make a lot of mistakes and I made my share."

School Funding for Democrats and Progressive Republicans

This essay will outline four long-term goals for the Democratic Party and for Progressive Republicans in Illinois. In thirty-five years of working with state legislators in many states, I am aware of how difficult it is to achieve the goals that are herein advocated. Many compromises and a lot of legislative tactics will be required to meet these goals. However, it is necessary to have a general road map for this is an area in which it is easy to lose one's way.

The third President of the United States, Thomas Jefferson, is usually credited with founding the Democratic Party. It seems appropriate to start with him. Mr. Jefferson was a man of prodigious intellect. His knowledge ran from philosophy and history through architecture and agriculture. He was also knowledgeable of school funding. When he was Governor of Virginia, he recommended an entire educational system to the Virginia legislature. Shortly before he died in the early 1820s, he reviewed what the Virginia legislature had done. He noted that, contrary to his recommendation that the state pick up the entire costs of K-12 education, they had left this tax burden to the individual school districts. He said in essence that the system would not work. The wealthy districts would have good schools and the poor districts would have bad schools. Nothing has changed since Mr. Jefferson's evaluation. The system still does not work.

Inequalities between school districts are dependent on a number of factors. If a state is geographically large, if it has many school districts, if it has a history of large economic differences within the state and if it also has a history of low state support and high local support, there will be large inequalities in educational services between school districts. Unfortunately, Illinois is just such a state. The result has been that disparities between school districts within Illinois are some of the largest in the Union, at least where the so-called "dual districts" are concerned. (In Illinois, Dual Districts are public school districts which offer only elementary grades or only secondary grades.) Unit districts do not show quite this large disparity.

Since the Democratic Party of Illinois is committed to equal educational opportunity, a long-term goal of the Party should be to reduce these inequalities between school districts. This situation is often referred to in school finance jargon as the "equity" problem. The solution to the equity problem is to move from largely local support to largely state support of education. This means higher state taxes and lower local property taxes. A part of this can come in the form of property tax relief provided the state government makes up dollar for dollar what is proposed as property tax relief. It is also possible to reduce this disparity with property tax caps on local school districts provided state funds are allowed to increase at the same time. A reduction in disparities can also be obtained by reducing the number of districts in the state, especially by merging dual districts into unit districts.

A second goal of the Democratic Party is to secure "adequate" funding as well as "equitable" funding. In some states, this is made easier by a state constitution that mandates that all citizens of the state receive an "adequate" or "basic" education. Regrettably, Illinois is not one of those states. In 1994, in *The Committee v. Edgar*, the Supreme Court of Illinois declared that the present Article Ten of the Illinois Constitution does not provide the citizens of this state with a fundamental right to education. Education was declared to be a major state interest, but not a fundamental constitutional right. Two years previously, in 1992, educational groups, with the considerable assistance of the Democratic Party and Progressive Republicans, had tried to amend Article Ten so that it would provide citizens with a fundamental right to an adequate education. Amendments to the constitution require sixty percent of those voting to pass; the amendment failed by only a few percentage points. The amendment failed largely because of business groups' opposition to the increase in state taxes that would be necessary in order to attain an "adequate" level of funding for education. Within the next few years, it would seem appropriate for the Democratic Party and for Progressive Republicans to again attempt a constitutional referendum that would guarantee all of the citizens of Illinois a fundamental right to an adequate education.

A third long-term goal of the Democratic Party and of Progressive Republicans is to attain economic efficiency in the public schools of Illinois. This can be done in a number of ways. First, it has been apparent for some time that there are too many school districts in this state. Consolidation and reorganization would produce economies of scale that could be passed on to taxpayers. This is not a popular thing to do. Consolidations can often lose state legislators more votes than they can possibly attain. Small towns fight effectively to keep their public schools even though they know those schools are economically inefficient. Second, related to size, no public school ought to operate without a full time business manager. If it proves impossible to merge districts, a full time business manger should be shared between schools. Third, both the business and educational practices of districts that operate with higher than expected test scores, at lower than expected costs, should be rigorously inspected to see how they arrive at that favorable product/cost ratio.

The conservative side of the aisle says little about the "equity" or "adequacy" problems. They have much to say about the "efficiency" goal. They advocate voucher systems, Charter Schools, and other privatization systems for what is now public education. Most of these proposals would, unfortunately, make the "equity" problem worse, because almost all of these systems would increase educational disparities between school districts. Both voucher systems and Charter Schools are means of skimming off the better students while leaving behind the poorer students. Proponents of these systems rarely address the question of what happens to those left behind in the "public schools." Nor do these systems address very well the question of who is to educate the disabled children in the society. Since it gives priority to equalizing educational opportunity, the Democratic Party and Progressive Republicans should oppose most of these privatization schemes. Proposals to increase competition within the public sector should be supported.

A fourth long-term goal of the Democratic Party is to secure adequate funds for children at risk. Spending the same amount of money on each child does not attain the first goal, "equity." Children with physical and mental disabilities require more funds than do other children

Also, children raised in poverty environments require more funds than do other children. It must honestly be said that it is questionable whether educational spending in the central cities and sparsely populated rural areas of Illinois can ever be "economically efficient" in the usually accepted sense of that term. In many central city environments and in some rural environments, the proper analogy is an "intensive care" ward. "ICU" is engaged in saving lives, not in delivering health care in the most economically efficient manner. Exactly the same situation holds in many of the worst educational environments in Illinois. There, schools are engaged in saving kids' lives and futures and not in doing that in the most economical way possible. It is very hard to find that "bottom line" in special education and compensatory education.

These four goals constitute a long-term strategy for the Democratic Party, but it is a rock bottom fact that they cannot be attained in Illinois without Republican help. Fortunately, there have always been enough Republicans who agreed with these goals and have been willing to support them, even though legislation of this kind did not always help the constituencies that these Republicans represented. Educators in Illinois may well owe more to these few, important and courageous Republicans, than they do to Democrats. At the national, level men like Robert Taft and Wendell Wilkie never considered educational spending in the same light as other public expenditures. They considered it an investment in the nation. Republicans, as well as Democrats, do respond to the principle of the greatest good for the greatest number.

Men like Jefferson, Franklin, Madison, Lincoln, Wilson, T. Roosevelt, F. D. Roosevelt, and John Kennedy all knew what public education means to this democracy. In any age or time, under any set of circumstances, it is the responsibility of Democrats and Progressive Republicans to rally to the support of the public schools. Be advised that in Illinois we have done, and we intend to do, just that.

Taxation, Politics and Education

"Taxation" is a fighting word. We fought a revolutionary war over the subject of taxation without representation. This was a war that the great conservative, Edmund Burke, (there are great Conservatives) said could have been avoided if the Colonials had been given ten seats in Parliament. No less than Benjamin Franklin agreed, at least up to just before the shots were fired at Concord Bridge. We fight over the amount of taxation, the level of government at which taxation should take place, and the tax instruments that should accomplish this taxation. We agree that taxation must take place. Illinois Governors as diverse as Adlai Stevenson and Big Jim Thompson have said that taxation is the price of civilization.

We have our usual battle lines. Liberals generally want more taxation and Conservatives less taxation. During the Reagan Administration, American Conservatives made one of the smartest changes in American politics. Rather than continue to oppose more public services, as they had since the Roosevelt era, they changed to opposing the collection of revenues, which support those services. This has served them very well politically, but has caused considerable damage to the national debt. Generally, Conservatives would rather see taxation at the state and local levels than at the national level. Conservatives also favor sales or consumption taxes, while Liberals favor income taxes. Conservatives oppose inheritance taxes, while Liberals favor them. Conservatives favor a flat rate tax; Liberals favor a "progressive" or graduated rate tax.

Is any agreement possible in this highly contentious area? Yes, by turning to factual data you can sometimes get a modicum of agreement. On both sides in the Illinois General Assembly it has been known for decades that Illinois property taxes are higher than many states and that Illinois state income taxes are lower than many other states. There appears to be agreement that a "tax switch" which would simultaneously lower the property tax and increase the income tax would be a good thing. Why doesn't this happen?

A big part of the difficulty here lies in school finance. As the late Professor Charles Benson used to say, "School finance is that twilight zone where accounting meets smoke and mirrors." It is the largest single state expenditure in many states. It is complicated by history. In the beginning of public education in Illinois, all expenses for the common schools were borne by the state government. However, as the 19th Century closed, those expenditures were transferred to the local governments. With the establishment of high schools in Illinois, the state began to help again with the expenditures for the K-12 schools. Many states support public education from state revenues more heavily than does Illinois. This stubborn reluctance to move off the local property tax base for public education has caused all kinds of problems.

Jump to the present time. The worst kept secret in Illinois politics is that the state taxes will have to be raised when the present bloodletting stops from cutting the state budget. Enter then the possible timing for this much needed switch. The property taxes could be frozen for a three-year period of time and income taxes could simultaneously be raised. Granted, this is a temporary solution because no taxes can be kept permanently frozen, but it would be a strong step in the right direction. There would be an immediate objection from the Superintendents of School Districts, and rightly so, because that would put an intolerable burden on the wealthier suburban school districts which receive little state aid. Since the early 1920s, the state aid distribution formula has given more state money to the property poor districts and less to the property wealthy districts.

The state distribution formula, however, is not carved in stone. In fact, that happens to be the most amended portion of the entire *School Code*. The formula can be changed so that the suburban school districts receive some additional state aid during this period of a proposed property tax moratorium. This could be done by a sharp increase in the foundation level of the state aid formula. This might appear to short change poor kids in the short run, but it would be beneficial to poor kids in the longer run. The property tax is the most unpopular tax we have, largely because consumption and income taxes are partially withheld at the source; thus, are partially "invisible" to the payer. As long as we depend primarily on the property taxes, we will never fund the K-12 schools either adequately or equitably.

Will everyone be happy with this solution? Not by a long shot. It would change the "incidence" of taxation, that is, the burden of taxation would fall on different kinds of taxpayers from what it does at present. But, this is one form of "change" that some Conservatives as well as some Liberals might support. In this state, as in many others, you cannot legislate anything without support from both sides. That is just what the Founding Fathers had in mind.

Taxation Reform:
Key to Education Funding Crisis

"These are times that try men's souls. This is no time for the summer patriot and the sunshine soldier," said Thomas Paine. You could say as much for the current educational funding crisis in Illinois. Over 80% of the school districts face budget shortfalls and many will be required to eliminate programs and lay off teachers.

Why do we have this problem and what can we do about it? Governor Blagojevich thinks we have this problem due to economic inefficiency; the State Superintendent thinks we have this problem due to lack of political will to do anything about the problem. They are both right.

We did not stumble into this miserable swamp overnight. Our first major mistake goes all the way back to 1970. The Constitutional Convention of that year deadlocked over the Revenue Article. One group wanted no income tax and one group wanted a progressive income tax (higher rates on the wealthy). The result was an adjusted flat rate tax, which is now clearly shown to be of insufficient yield to finance modern state government. We should have stayed the course for a progressive income tax. The result is that Illinois is one of only nine states to struggle along with a flat rate income tax. Currently, we have the lowest rate in the nation, except for Pennsylvania. We can still have a progressive income tax, but it would take a constitutional amendment to put one in place.

The second major mistake was slowly to shift the tax burden of the public schools from the state government to the local government. After several decades, Illinois reached a point where the state government was actually providing just short of half the funds to run the public schools. Then, began a long, slow retreat from that position with the result that the local property tax payers had to pick up more and more of the tab. Interestingly, most states were going in exactly the other direction when Illinois began this perverse journey. Property tax caps stayed this shift somewhat. The shift has also been greatly slowed by failed local referenda. So, what can we do about it?

First, reverse the shift. Freeze the property taxes for education at their current level for at least three years. Simultaneously, increase the personal income tax by one percent (move from 3% to 4%) and earmark that tax increase for education. Some adjustments in the state aid distribution formula would have to be made since this move shuts off wealthy school districts from local revenue increases for a period of time.

Second, since the federal government has moved partially off the estate tax (also called inheritance tax and death tax) the state should move rapidly into that slot. There needs to be a high exemption here, perhaps as high as three million dollars, so that farmers and small businessmen will not be caught when their assets pass from one generation to the next. Also, that rate should be progressive so that the heaviest burden falls on the wealthiest estates. There is a sense of poetic justice here, taxing the plutocracy in favor of the meritocracy.

Third, review the sales tax to see if a small increase is possible after exemptions have been put in place for food and medicine. This well might be a "luxury" tax falling only on items above a certain dollar amount.

Fourth, the British government is currently exploring the possibility of local income taxes to support some of their local government services. We should as well. However, a local option income tax to support education would have to be accompanied by a change in the state aid formula, otherwise the school districts with strong income bases would simply run off and leave the income poor districts.

Fifth, we need to think "outside of the box" on revenue matters. The bottom line here is that the current revenue system is fit for horse and buggy days. It has to be reformed. Some states get revenue from severance taxes on oil, gas, etc. Illinois could levy a severance tax on coal shipped out of the state, but hesitated to go in that direction because the soft coal industry was so weak. Perhaps we need to think of a severance tax on agricultural products.

Governor Blagojevich is not totally off base with his search for economic efficiency. However, the most inefficient school finance matter is well known to everyone. That is the fact that we have about a third more school districts than we need. We have known about these diseconomies of scale for decades.

Oliver Wendell Holmes was right, "Taxation is the price of Civilization." The late Paul Simon was also right, "Don't ask for these services unless you are ready to pay for them."

Is Ricardo Still Right?

Early in the 19th Century, David Ricardo formulated the theory of comparative advantage. In essence, that theory says that, when each nation is allowed to produce what it can most efficiently and is allowed to trade that product freely with other countries, all nations will be better off. In these days of "outsourcing, insourcing, and off shoring," is the theory still sound?

A recent book by Thomas L. Friedman, *The World is Flat*, argues that Ricardo is still right, subject to some big qualifications. The book is crammed full of interesting data. We find, for example, that Wal-Mart has over 5000 independent suppliers on the east coast of China.

We find that Hewlett-Packard has 142,000 employees in 172 countries. Rolls Royce, while still headquartered in the United Kingdom, has the same international coverage. When you call for technical support for America online, that friendly voice that speaks in American slang with a slight accent is coming to you from Bangalore, India.

When NAFTA was before the Congress, Ross Perot warned of the big sucking sound that would be made by American jobs going south of the border. Mr. Perot got his geography wrong. That sound came from India where the more technical jobs go and from China where the manufacturing jobs go. Yes, this is a better world when those countries are better employed.

So, what do we do about displaced workers in the United States? Friedman thinks we can handle this with increased education and re-education of the American workforce. However, most states, including Illinois, are hard pressed to find enough funds for K-12 education, let alone to find the amount of funds that would have to go into higher education and to technological education to do what Friedman says should be done. One painfully recalls that in 1993, Illinois State University had to close its College of Continuing Education for lack of funding. If we are unwilling to tax for education, then we had better vote against NAFTA, CAFTA and other free trade agreements that come our way.

The Federal Role in Education

A decade ago, at the invitation of the late Paul Simon, I had the privilege of being the lead witness before the U.S. Senate Subcommittee on Education, Arts and Humanities. The Senate was investigating problems of school finance including especially the role of the federal government in school finance. For a superannuated professor, the probability of that happening again is not too likely. However, I have been wondering recently just what I would say, if I were to testify again.

I doubt that the central theme would be different now from what it was ten years ago. I would say that President Lyndon Johnson had set the federal government on a correct course when he sought to have the government rectify the differences in educational provision both between states and between school districts within a state. Also, his idea of having the federal government direct federal funds into poverty pockets, both within the large cities of the United States and in rural areas, was a sound investment strategy for this nation.

I would also testify, as I did then, that President Richard Nixon was also on the right course when, in 1973, he arranged for federal revenue sharing with the states. Many states, including Illinois, used those unexpected funds for educational purposes. In fact, it is the plain truth that the only time we made significant progress in reducing the difference between districts in expenditures per pupil was when those federal funds were available. I would again draw attention to legislation introduced by both former Senator Adlai Stevenson of Illinois and Representative David Obey of Wisconsin, which would reward states that reduced the educational expenditure differences between districts within a state.

Times change. We have other educational needs, which the federal government should now address. As I explained in my last commentary in the *Pantagraph*, we could increase our test scores by balancing the socio-economic composition of schools and requiring that no school may have over a majority of students from poverty homes. The federal government could pick up the expense of what bussing would be required to do this.

Bricks and mortar are always a cost; therefore, more could be done in the capital cost area. The federal government could provide a useful cost-effectiveness nudge here, if new school buildings built with federal funds could be used as an incentive for further school consolidation. Our provision for teaching in foreign languages and science is also beginning to lag again, so it is time to renew the National Defense Education Act that was passed in the Eisenhower Administration. The extreme shortage of Arabic speakers in the armed forces in Iraq is just the tip of the iceberg.

Hardly any economist, liberal or conservative, disagrees with the need to raise the educational level of the work force. It comes as a considerable shock for most of us to realize that Sweden, Finland and Ireland, have a better-educated work force than the USA. It also comes as a shock to find that Luxembourg and Norway are now wealthier, on average, than we are. Both Conservatives and Liberals agree that something must be done to upgrade the skills of workers who have been rendered unemployed by outsourcing of their jobs. There is an immediate and strong need for federal help in this area. Much of it should be directed to community colleges, which are better equipped than secondary schools to handle this adult and continuing education problem.

If we intend to live at peace with the rest of the world, there are a number of things that need to be done. We need to stress "multicultural" offerings in both secondary and tertiary education. Federal funds could help with that. We also need to expand scholarships for foreign students. What little good will we have left in this world is largely due to those students who remember how well they were treated when they were in the USA. We also need to help other countries, especially in the Middle East, expand their secular education offerings. Many of our foreign policy headaches today come from the fact that elementary and secondary education in the Middle East is run by extremists of the Muslim faith. It need not have been that way.

If we must have large armed forces for our safety, then the least we can do is provide a new G.I. Bill for those serving in both the active forces, the reserves and the National Guard. If we do not move on this very soon our "all volunteer" army could collapse causing us to face a draft as unpopular as it was during the Vietnam War.

All of the above policies would require an increase in federal investment in education. Unfortunately, we seem headed in the opposite direction. Some recent cuts in federal money to Illinois school districts are as follows: Bloomington, $100,000; Peoria, $718,000; East St. Louis, $271,500; North Chicago, $127,000; City of Chicago, $41,000,000. However, hope springs eternal. Matters could change after the next election.

School Vouchers:
Solution or Another Problem

Vouchers are not a new idea. Milton Friedman, a noted economist, advocated them in the late 1940s. Under the Friedman proposal, the state would provide a certificate worth a certain amount of money. The parents could then add to this amount from their own pockets and take the certificate to any school, private or public, and cash it in. Schemes like Friedman's general voucher have been proposed in many states, usually by referendum. They have succeeded in none. Why? Because they would clearly make the ancient equity problem much worse. The wealthy parent could spend much more than could the poor parent, and the differential between the rich and the poor schools would continue to grow.

Sometime in the 1950s, a counter proposal arose. Rather than a general voucher, as Friedman advocated, why not have a voucher inverse to wealth? Eventually, this became a notion of restricting the voucher to only poor parents. In that form, it has seen its way into law at least in Wisconsin and Ohio. Pro-voucher people believe this highly restricted voucher proposal may pass the scrutiny of the "establishment clause" in the first amendment.

About thirty years ago, in the last days of Governor Richard Ogilvie's administration, an Illinois school finance task force recommended a "voucher to the poor" system. It was not accepted for the following reasons. First, as George Will, a voucher advocate, candidly admitted in a *Pantagraph* column, "Suburban public schools refuse to receive poor, inner-city scholarship students." It was believed they would continue to do so under a voucher system. Since that time, the British have adopted a system of scholarships to their elite private schools that required those schools to reserve a percentage of their seats for low-income scholars. Thirty years ago, few were prepared to require both public and private schools in Illinois to reserve a quota of seats for the poor. Are they now?

Much discussion ensued at that time over the alleged, "creaming off effect." School officials thought that the better students would take advantage of the vouchers and thus leave behind the low-income students in the inner-city schools. The disappearance of good role models in the student population would have a negative effect on those who were left behind. It has been well established that the single most powerful variable in predicting test scores in a given school is the percentage of children from low-income families in that school; the greater the percentage of low-income children, the lower the test scores. Since a voucher system would likely remove students from middle-income parents, the percentage of students from low-income parents would increase and the average test scores of the "left behinds" would, according, decline drastically.

Another matter of concern was the schooling of disabled children. These students are costly to educate; therefore, it was felt that many schools would not voluntarily take students with physical or mental disabilities. There was also the matter of transportation. Since the children of the poor generally lack transportation, the state would have to shoulder extra costs in bussing the "vouchered children" to their new schools. There was also the matter of social exclusion in the receiving school brought on by differences in clothing and in speech habits of the poor. Perhaps, if all students wore uniforms, as they do in many British schools, it might work, but American schools have largely opposed school uniforms. Finally, the voucher proposals would take the future leaders of minorities from their natural base and inculcate them in the values of the white middle class. Well-educated minority leaders already have major problems in communicating with their less-well-educated rank and file population and the "voucher to the poor" would likely make that gap worse.

Finally, for those of us who still believe that every student in this state has a fundamental right to an adequate education, vouchers are merely another "save a few by sacrificing the many" proposal. Nuts!!

A Mistake Corrected:
A Note on Cost Effectiveness

[Editorial Note: The 2005 *Yearbook* of the American Education Finance Association reviews current research on economic efficiency in school finance.]

While further research would be needed to prove this point, it is not unlikely that the practice of balancing the socio-economic composition of students in schools could turn out to be a cost effective way to raise test scores in the public schools. The standard approach to raising test scores of children from poor homes is to reduce the pupil-teacher ratio in those classes, or to add teacher aides to those classes. This has been shown to be effective in raising test scores, but the cost is high. Even if it were necessary to add costs from bussing students those costs would likely not be as high as adding teaching personnel. If the scores rise just as much by reducing the percentage of children at risk in the school below fifty percent, then this is also the least costly way to raise scores.

About two decades ago, I headed a research team that reported to the then existing Illinois School Problems Commission. We were investigating the causes of low test scores in the public schools. We found that the leading cause of poor test scores was the percentage of students from families below the poverty line in a given school. We also found that a "tipping point" existed, so that, when there were more than a majority of poverty-impacted pupils, the test scores in the school fell like a rock. Since then, this finding has been replicated many places in the United States, in Great Britain and in Japan.

The policy recommendation that my colleague, Ben Hubbard, and I made to the General Assembly at that time was that the weighting in the grant-in-aid formula for poverty students should be increased for districts with high concentrations of these kinds of pupils. The recommendation was accepted; the law was accordingly changed; and more state money flowed to poverty-impacted schools. I received an award from the Urban League of Chicago for my role in that endeavor. Our diagnosis was correct. However, with the passage of time, I have come to believe that the therapy we suggested was not nearly aggressive enough. What I should have recommended was that NO public school be allowed to operate with more than a majority of students from poverty families. Of course, to attain these goals would require help from the state in terms of drawing new attendance lines and in the bussing of students.

Bussing students is assuredly not popular, even to obey the edicts of the court, as in *Brown v. the Board*. In the fifty years since *Brown*, we have learned that not only is racial segregation bad for the schools, but also socio-economic segregation is even worse. Therefore, to insist rigorously on "neighborhood schools" often condemns some students to a bad education and gives other students a good education. Granted, this situation is not as bad in places like Bloomington/Normal as it is in the larger metropolitan areas where there are both schools and school districts with no poverty students and other schools and districts in which every student comes from a poverty home.

Why admit the mistake now? Because socio-economic segregation in American schools is growing decade by decade. A large number of economic studies indicate that both wealth and income are now more concentrated than they have been since 1890 and 1920. These inequalities in wealth and income become translated into very unequal residential housing choices. People use their wealth to choose homes that will also provide good schools for their children. Very understandable. But the poor are unable to do that. In a private enterprise system, the people surely have every right to choose automobiles, clothing, and, yes, housing on the basis of their individual purchasing power in the market. But at least in my opinion, they do not, have a right to exert this differential purchasing power with regard to public schools. The public schools, unlike some private schools, are not a commodity to be purchased on the free market. The "Common Schools" are exactly that. They exist for the greatest good for the greatest number.

All this has been known for a very long time. It is very disturbing to most people to be forced to look at this problem. Why not just sweep it all under a rug? Because the stakes are now much higher than they were a quarter of a century ago. Most economists, liberal or conservative, agree that our economy cannot survive in this competitive world without greatly increasing the effectiveness of the public schools. We did not really become alarmed about this until middle class jobs started to disappear to South America, the Far East and to Europe. We must do something and do it fast. Without effective schools, our mighty armed forces will not work, our highly technical economy will not work, our medical services will not work and, it is for darned certain, our democracy will not work. Certain kinds of charter schools, and even a very carefully controlled voucher system might help, but they would just be band-aids on a major infection. Additionally, an uncontrolled voucher system could very well make the disease worse.

This is not the pipe dream of a superannuated professor from Illinois State University. A remarkably good book published recently from the Brookings Institution lays out much of the research on this issue. It also provides examples of school districts that have faced the problem squarely and have done something about it. Ever the teacher, I suggest you add Richard D. Kahlenberg's, *All Together Now*, 2001, to your reading list.

Unit Five School Board Shows Guts

Membership on a School Board is one of the many thankless, difficult jobs that must be done to make a democracy work. When it is done well, it surely should be noted. McLean County Unit District Five's attempt to balance the percentage of children from low socio-economic families among its various school jurisdictions is based on solid sociological and educational research. Tons of studies show that the single most important predictor of low test scores is the percentage of children from low-income families in the jurisdiction. The greater the percentage of lower-income students in a jurisdiction, the lower the test scores. Therefore, it is solid public policy to make this percentage as even as possible between jurisdictions.

Unfortunately, there are limits on how much can be done here since the largest differences are usually between elementary jurisdictions, so proximity is a major consideration with younger children. Ultimately, the critics of the balancing policy are also right about one thing. It is segregation by social class that is the prime cause of this problem. The rich live together; the poor live together; and they both put as much geographic space between one another as they possibly can. Sociological studies of this problem go back over 75 years, usually under the title of "urban ecology."

The Unit Five School Board is following the utilitarian premise of "the greatest good for the greatest number." Unfortunately, when the greatest good for most children is NOT the same as the greatest good for your child, there is a real emotional twist. The middle class school board member voting for a policy that will not particularly help middle class children has a stronger sense of citizenship than most of us possess.

There is one saving grace. That same body of research shows that the percentage needs to be greater than 50% to have a strong negative influence on test scores. Most jurisdictions in Unit 5 have not yet reached that point. If the Board does not buckle under pressure, and holds to its course, it will deserve a "profiles in courage" award.

Privatization of Education: A Mistake

Jason Wright's recent guest commentary in the *Pantagraph* is off base on several matters. He argues that public education is not economically efficient and should be abandoned in favor of private education. We shall answer this in two parts. In the first part, we shall argue that there is evidence that public education is economically efficient. In the second part, we shall argue that, even if public education is not totally economically efficient, there are good and sufficient reasons why education should remain in public hands.

Using relatively crude research from the American Legislative Exchange Council, Wright points out that there is no relationship between what is spent on education and educational outcomes. Much of this type of research is flawed. It is flawed because it fails to control for the different kinds of students in the different kinds of districts before the effects of spending are related to the educational outcomes. Research that does control, in advance, for the different kinds of children shows that there is a small, but positive, relationship between what is spent and educational outcomes. These studies can be obtained through the Graduate School of Education at Harvard University.

The reason that the relationship between what is spent and what is received is so small can be easily understood by looking at any two districts in Illinois. Let us take the McLean County Unit District 5 and the Chicago school district. Chicago has a higher level of spending than Unit 5, but it also has lower test scores than Unit 5. Of course, they do. Chicago needs to spend a good deal more money to offset the effects of high levels of poverty in the homes of its students than does Unit 5. But this is no indication of the economic inefficiency of public education in

Illinois. Those extra funds are needed in Chicago just to try to achieve a level playing field. It is akin to the fact that expenditures in intensive care wards in hospitals are always higher than they are in regular wards. The low rate of return on investment is exactly what you would expect when you are trying to equalize educational opportunity between quite disparate groups of students, rather than increasing the overall student output at the lowest cost.

The reasons for offering education on a public basis rather than a private basis, however, have never been primarily economic in nature. They are political and sociological and are of quite ancient origin. In the Fourth Book of the *Politics,* Aristotle argued that a City State with a strong middle class was much more stable than a City State with many citizens who were rich and many citizens who were poor. Jefferson and Franklin both argued that this strong middle class could only be obtained by a common school education that was available to all citizens. Privatizing education might result in some very good schools, but those good schools would not be available to the poor and the disabled. Therefore, privatization of education would contribute greatly to the increasing inequality in income in the United States and would ultimately destroy the middle class, replacing it with large concentrations of rich and poor.

The public schools serve many valuable sociological functions that cannot be served by private education. We are a multiracial and multicultural society. We must have an institution that provides the glue that holds this conglomerate society together. That institution is the public schools that provide us with shared cultural values that are passed from generation to generation. Without that glue, we could not long survive. Mr. Wright never saw the fires burning in Chicago in the 1960s, but I did. I was there. I never want to see them again. No private educational system can handle the diversity that is now the United States.

The public schools also provide us with the "upward mobility" needed in a democracy. Foreign observers like De Tocqueville and Baron Acton have always pointed to the public education system as THE distinctive element in American democracy. Unlike the society of "old Europe," this was a society, which allowed a Lincoln to move from a log cabin to the White House. I, for one, do not want to live in a country in which the leadership is drawn only from elite private schools, even though I hold two degrees from Harvard University.

The final argument for public education is simply the survival of the United States. Without the public schools, the impressive military might of this country would fail. A private education system might produce a lot of intelligent officers, but it could not produce the number of intelligent enlisted men needed to carry out their orders. Nor can a private education system produce an educated labor force to compete with other nations. Without a skilled labor force we would be quickly reduced to the level of a third world power.

Leaving the United States Constitutional Convention, a woman asked Benjamin Franklin what kind of government they had given the people. Eighty-one year-old Ben replied, "A Republic, if you can keep it." Well, you can't keep it without a good public education.

Governor's Cure Worse
Than the Disease

Governor Blagojevich's well-intended educational reform is wrong on several counts. In the first place, Section Two of Article Ten of the Illinois Constitution clearly places the responsibility for selecting the State Superintendent in the hands of the State Board of Education. To get around this "constitutional inconvenience," the Governor proposes to create a Department of Education with an appointed Secretary. However, since there is no constitutional amendment contemplated, this would leave in place the original Board of Education and presumably the original Superintendent, as well. That is a most inefficient and uneconomical way to handle the perceived, and often real, problems of the State Board.

Much sounder is the proposal of the Illinois School Boards Association (ISBA) to elect the State Board of Education. Two states, Utah and Hawaii, do that on a non-partisan ballot. Two other systems, Ohio and Washington, D.C., elect part of the Board and appoint the other part. The ISBA proposal can be carried out without a constitutional amendment since Section Two of Article Ten also says the Board can be "elected or selected." This is a preferable way to make the Board "more accountable."

The members of the Constitutional Convention of 1970 (and 1870, for that matter) did not want to have education provided by the Governor's appointees. To do so would be to invite partisan political appointments rather than professional educational appointments. If you think that the present department of Secretary of State should serve as a "role model" for education, you surely are thinking differently from many of us. A far more courageous posture would be to amend the constitution to assure a fundamental right to an adequate education. We came very close to doing exactly that in 1992.

Give this to the Governor Blagojevich: at least he is trying to lead in educational reform, which few in that office have done since the late Governor Ogilvie. However, using the Board of Education as a general scapegoat is simply not the way to do it.

House Bill 750

In the *Pantagraph's* "Our Views" of April 29th, regarding HB750, the editorial states: "Although the proposal would provide the immediate infusion of cash educators want, it doesn't address the key issue: Keeping spending growth in line with revenue growth." I would answer that one should worry about keeping spending in line with revenue growth only when that revenue growth has been shown to be adequate in the past. Educational revenue growth has not been adequate in Illinois because the tax system itself is so badly structured.

For over three decades, we have pounded and pounded and pounded at the point that dependence on the property tax is too great and dependence on the sales and income taxes is not enough. Yes, that criticism IS bipartisan in nature. In the past, proposals by both Dawn Clark Netsch (Democrat) and Aldo DeAngelo (Republican) put this issue squarely at the center of the legislative reforms they recommended, just as does this current proposal from the bipartisan Center for Tax and Budget Accountability.

The fact is that it will never be possible to fund education in Illinois either adequately or equitably without first correcting this imbalance in the tax structure. You point to the "stability" of the property tax yield. You are correct. That yield is not only "stable," but also is regrettably insufficiently elastic. That is, it does not move adequately with inflation; therefore, cannot keep pace with rising costs. The yields from the sales and income taxes are much more elastic; they can keep pace with rising costs. If we were overly dependent on the sales and income taxes, then a danger, which the editorial correctly points out, might exist in the event of a major recession or depression. In such a situation, revenues for education would fall rapidly. Presently, we find ourselves far from that situation.

I support this bill strongly, but I am aware that it does not address the needs of disabled and poverty impacted students. I assume these omissions will be explored as the debate progresses.

Added Note to HB750: The *Pantagraph's* editorial of June 7, 2005, tells us that, once again, the attempt to shift educational funding from the property tax to the income tax has failed. The Meeks/Winkle initiative failed just as so many other attempts have failed in the past. Since the major political opposition always arises in the same part of the state, the wealthy Chicago suburbs, it is almost impossible not to conclude that Representatives and Senators from that area like the system just as it is.

Of course, they do. They have good public schools supported by their high property valuations and, to their credit, supported by their higher than expected property tax rates. They do not receive much general state aid, although they do receive considerable categorical state aid. What would shake their complacency? Well, if the bubble ever bursts on the residential valuations, that might put them in a different position. Tougher property tax extension limitations might also do it. A general depression, brought on by the collapse of the dollar, certainly would. But really, how do you combat an ideology that says, "I've got mine; now pull up the ladder."

Outline of Prospective Legislation for an Annual Equity Report

For almost a quarter of a century, the Center for the Study of Educational Finance at Illinois State University documented the progress of the State of Illinois toward or away from equality of educational opportunity. In the early days, the Center's reports went to the School Problems Commission and later directly to the Governor and the General Assembly. Due to retirements and budget problems, this function has been dropped in recent years. Some of us feel it is a task that is too important to abandon. Accordingly, I have drafted this proposal, which would require the State of Illinois and State Board of Education to take over this function. Although the number of legislators with an interest in equity may not be as great as in the past, hopefully, enough remain to see this into law.

Such a bill would read as follows: Inasmuch as it is a goal of the General Assembly of Illinois to achieve equality of educational opportunity, the Superintendent of Education is directed to transmit to the General Assembly and to the Governor an Annual Equity Report, which shall contain, but not be limited to, the following information.

1. The variance among the school districts with regard to: (a) operating expenditures per pupil; (b) property valuation per pupil; (c) educational tax rate; (d) general state aid per pupil; (e) categorical state aid per pupil; (f) median family income; and (g) test results on all academic achievement tests required by the state. Standard statistical descriptive measures shall be used, including the standard deviation and the coefficient of variation. When a sufficient number of annual measurements

have been taken, a time series of these measurements shall be established so that the General Assembly shall know whether the state has been moving in the direction of equality of educational opportunity or away from equality of educational opportunity. These measurements shall be supplemented by cartographic analysis so that regional inequalities may be studied.

2. The Annual Equity Report shall also state the association of these variables: (a) property valuation per pupil and expenditure per pupil; (b) median family income and expenditure per pupil; (c) median family income and test scores; (d) property valuation per pupil and general state aid per pupil; and (e) median family income and categorical state aid. Standard statistical descriptive measures shall be used, including the product moment correlation coefficient and the standardized regression coefficient. When a sufficient number of annual measurements have been established, a time series shall be established so that the General Assembly shall know whether educational provision and outcomes are becoming a greater function of local wealth or whether they are becoming less of a function of local wealth.

3. The Annual Equity Report shall also state what actions have been taken by the State Superintendent and the State Board to reduce the variance in educational expenditures and educational outcomes between school districts and what actions have been taken to reduce the relationship of local wealth to educational expenditures and outcomes. The Report shall also state the cost and effectiveness of these actions.

4. The Annual Equity Report may be prepared in house or the Report may be contracted out to acknowledged experts in school finance, or both, provided that the external contract does not exceed $40,000 in any given fiscal year. The budget of the State Superintendent shall reflect this as a separate item.

5. The Report shall be printed and published by the State Board of Education and shall be distributed to all members of the General Assembly and the Executive Office of the Governor. An executive summary shall be made available to the media.

Significant Dates in Illinois School Finance

1820: Thomas Jefferson introduces a full state funding proposal in Virginia; Jefferson declares the system adopted by the House of Burgesses (all local funding) to be "unworkable."

1850's: The Whigs (including Abraham Lincoln) establish a public school system in Illinois. Initially fully state funded; the system rapidly becomes locally funded with the state's contribution limited to a low flat grant per pupil.

1890: By this date, the state system is mostly locally funded.

1927: Illinois adopts a Foundation Level (Strayer-Haig) system of funding which distributes state aid inversely to property tax wealth. Significant increase in state support.

1930: Several local systems fail in the great depression.

Professor Henry Morrison (U. of Chicago) condemns the Illinois system of state and local funding as "appropriate for horse and buggy days" and advocates full state assumption.

1969: Passage of first state income tax. Significant increase in educational funding.

Article Ten is adopted in the Illinois Constitution. Failure to include education as a fundamental right. Failure to specify full state assumption. Revenue Article limits state to a flat rate income tax guaranteeing permanent shortage of education funding.

1971: *Serrano v. Priest* decided in California. Failure to file similar suit in Illinois

Three "Blue Ribbon" Committees for Educational Finance. Majority in one of these favors full state assumption

Hubbard/Hickrod formula adopted for state. Formula guarantees that districts with equal tax rates will have equal expenditures per pupil. Considered an answer to *Serrano*. This is largest increase in recent history in state funding. Part of this increase is due to Federal Revenue Sharing (Nixon Administration).

Hickrod poverty weighting adopted based on concentration of poverty in district.

1984: State returns to the Strayer/Haig. Prior formula thought to raise local property taxes too much. Poverty weighting retained.

1989: State Income Tax increased to 3.0 percent, results in significant increase in education funding.

1991: Legislative Task Force recommends property tax relief but fails to pass. County option Property Tax Extension (PTELL) first placed into formula.

1992: Attempt to amend Article Ten to include the statement; "a fundamental right to an adequate education" fails on close vote largely due to opposition by Governor Jim Edgar.

1994: *The Committee v. Edgar* is decided (6-1) for defendant. Supreme Court declares that education is NOT a constitutional right in Illinois.

Dawn Clark Netsch makes substitution of income tax for property tax a part of her gubernatorial race and is defeated. Professor Hickrod appears as the lead witness before a select committee of the United States Senate investigating problems in school finance.

1996: Senator Aldo DeAngelo (R) introduces bill to substitute income tax for property tax. Bill passes the Illinois House but fails in Senate. Governor's Commission on Educational Funding recommends separate categorical for poverty grant and higher foundation level.

1998: Poverty weighting removed from the general grant, where it had been since 1974 and made a separate categorical grant. Grade level weightings also removed from general grant.

1999: Adjustments placed in formula to reflect the effect of county option property tax extension limitation (PTELL)

2002: Educational Finance Advisory Board recommends a method of calculating Foundation Formula based upon earlier economic efficiency research at Illinois State University and the Professor Augenblick's Report. Also recommends change in poverty impaction grant. Consolidation of categorical grants.

2003: HB750 developed by the Center for Tax and Budget Accountability.

2004: Gifted categorical grant removed.

2005: Senator James Meeks and Senator Rick Winkle advance their version of a "tax swap" bill based on HB750.

Section IV

"Those who do not know the past are condemned to repeat it."

—Santayana

IV. War and the Iraq Conflict

A. Iraq: The Way Out

B. Iraq: One More Step in *Pax Americana*

C. Looting of the Baghdad National Museum

D. Wrong War, in the Wrong Way, at the Wrong Time

E. Wrong War Dangerous to Home Defense

F. Support Guards and Reservists

G. Good Wars/Bad Wars

H. War is Hell, But Madness May be Useful

I. The Corps: A Critical Assessment

J. This Time, No Tricks

Iraq: The Way Out

"All Gaul is divided into three parts," said Caesar. So is Iraq. The Bush Administration keeps speaking of an "Iraqi people." Hogwash, no such "people" exist and they never have existed. The Ottoman Empire divided that area into three provinces. One was administered from Mosul, a second from Baghdad, and a third from Basra. Each had a Turkish garrison and each was ruled by a Pasha; that is, a Turkish military governor.

When the Ottoman Empire was defeated in World War I, the victorious Allies established their Arab followers in Baghdad, as they did in most major cities of the Ottoman Empire outside of Turkey. They brought a Hashemite Prince, in their army baggage train, to rule over this heterogeneous and restless area. When that monarchy was overthrown by a group of young Arab Army officers, a military oligarchy held the area together. The civilian facet of this military group was the Baath Party. Saddam Hussein rose through the ranks of this military oligarchy until he became absolute dictator.

All analogies are imperfect, but you can think of Iraq as much like the Balkans. When the Austro-Hungarian Empire fell after World War I, several separate countries were created from that old empire. Many of these countries were not much more than geographic expressions, which contained irreconcilable ethnic groups.

After World War II, many of these areas fell under the control of Communism and under the hegemony of the Soviet Union. A strong military regime in Yugoslavia under Tito held the lid on ethnic conflict. In time, however, communist control was overthrown and all the old divisions of religion, nationalism and culture reappeared.

Elimination of Saddam Hussein has caused similar conflicts to reappear. In the north, the Kurds have an army of over 75,000 men eager to establish their long held dream of an independent Kurdistan. They will lay immediate claim to Kirkuk and the adjacent oil fields. They may also try to seize Mosul, but that may prove more difficult. In the south, the Shiite Muslims have strong military militias ready to establish a theocracy like neighboring Iran. This would not necessarily be simply a part of Iran, because this part of the world is Arab, not Persian. The conflict between Arab and Persian goes back into antiquity.

In the center, are the Sunni Arabs. Again, analogies are often imperfect, but think of Northern Ireland. The Sunnis are the Protestants and the Shiites are the Catholics. The Sunnis have lorded it over the Shiites for generations, but the Sunnis are in a minority. The Sunnis play a major part in the resistance to American occupation because they know that their future is grim in a Shiite controlled Iraq. The center of Iraq is the major problem area since Shiites are not likely to allow the Sunnis to reestablish their power again.

The way out may be to establish a very loose confederation of the three parts of Iraq. That is what a number of authors of papers in recent issues of *Foreign Affairs* seem to think. But, if that does not work, we should cut the Gordian knot and help the three parts to establish their own countries. As were the British in Palestine and in India after WWII, we are unfortunately stuck here until we can get these three groups on their own feet. Of the three parts, the only really pro-American part is Kurdistan. The Turks and the Iranians will certainly object to this, but the Turks also want to join the European Union and are unlikely to do anything more than fret publicly. However, if we do this, we had better be prepared to defend the Kurds against their several ancient enemies. Our record with the Armenians after World War I, our record in Vietnam, and our record with the Kurds against Saddam, do not recommend us as the staunchest and most valiant allies to have in this world.

Many feel that after a bloody civil war the Sunnis will simply be driven out and two countries will be left. A smaller Kurdistan will exist in the north and a much larger Shiite state will exist in the south. With considerable luck the southern Shiite theocracy might tilt our way to offset a rival Shiite theocracy in Iran. Neither of these states is likely ever to be a democracy. Given their long background of ethnic conflict and authoritarian control, it was an act of remarkable stupidity to think that would be the case.

This is a bloody mess. In its long run implications, it is worse than Vietnam. We now have much of the Arab world against us. Unless carefully handled, we could have the rest of the Islamic world against us as well. Some of these future adversaries have atomic weapons.

In naïve and childish ignorance, this administration has knocked over a wasp's nest, which will generate many more terrorists. It will make this country less safe for generations to come. The words of Santayana should absolutely ring in our ears: "Those who do not know the past are condemned to repeat it."

Iraq: One More Step in Pax Americana

When was it that we became policemen for the World? Was it in World War I when we made the world safe for democracy? Was it in World War II when we saved Western Civilization from another Dark Age? Was it in the Cold War? Was it in the Korean "Police Action"? Was it in our brave but confused intervention in Vietnam? Was it in another "police action" in Grenada? Was it in the first war with Iraq? Will it be in the second war with Iraq? No, this is not a plea for isolationism. "Fortress America" is stone cold dead in the market. The fact is we ARE the policemen of the modern world just as Rome was of the ancient world. For centuries, the Roman legions established and held the *Pax Romana*. Eventually, the strain of that effort broke them, just as the strain of supporting our world peace will probably break us; but we have no choice.

I am not smart enough to know WHY this cup came to us, but I think I know HOW it did. The *Washington Post* recently noted that when we established a military base outside of Tashkent in Central Asia, we were the first Western troops in that region of the world since Alexander the Great. We inherited the mantel of leadership from Alexander, who took it from Athens. Of course, it was a long time getting to us. Through the Roman Republic, through the Roman Empire, through the Renaissance City States, through Spain, through France and finally to England, it moved with relentless force. Then, when "Rule Britannica" mired down in the trenches of World War I, it started moving toward us. Like it or not, friends, we ARE the guardians of Western Civilization. With that comes the grim responsibility to keep order in this world. If my speculation is correct, we will hold this burden for a very long time. The Christians and other religions failed to establish the peace the way it should be done. So now, we hold it the way it has always been held, by the sword.

Looting of the Baghdad National Museum

The world of scholarship has sustained a colossal loss with the looting of the National Museum in Baghdad. Perhaps it does not rank with the burning of the library in Alexandria in ancient times, but it comes close. Gone are irreplaceable artifacts from Assyria and Babylon. Gone are the earliest known religious objects in historic times from Ur, the birthplace of Abraham, a patriarch unto Jews, Christians, and Muslims. In an unbelievable twist of fate, gone is the earliest legal document in the world, the Code of Hammurabi.

It appears that this act was carried out by mobs of poor Iraqis assisted by museum "insiders." However, we may have some culpability here. For months, scholars in the United States have pleaded with the Pentagon to spare the Museum. That may have worked since the building was not bombed or shelled. Just one platoon of Marines could have prevented this looting from occurring, but the Marines did not charge to the rescue in time. No man has more pride of Corps than I do. Maybe they ought to include a course in ancient history at Quantico. In recent weeks, the FBI has offered its services as has Interpol, but that is shutting the barn door after the horse is long gone.

Joint teams of reconstituted Baghdad Police and the 7th Marines now patrol the streets of Baghdad. This is dangerous work for Marines. Looters who are caught red-handed will try to gun their way out. It should be remembered that when fight we must, it is not only for this nation, but also for western civilization itself. The soldiers who stood against the Vandals, the Goths, the Vikings, the Huns, the Mongols, the Moors, the Turks and the Nazis, are equally as important as those who stood at Concord Bridge. Churchill as usual said it best, "Fail now and a new Dark Age will descend over the World, from which we may never recover."

Wrong War, in the Wrong Way, at the Wrong Time

With regret, this former Marine finds himself in opposition to the proposed war with Iraq for the following reasons:

First, this action will put in concrete a terrible constitutional mistake. James Madison and his colleagues assigned the right to declare war solely to Congress. They believed that vesting the Executive with that right was a danger to this Republic. For several decades, Presidents from both parties have edged the "war powers" away from Congress and into the hands of the Executive. Johnson did it with the Bay of Tonkin Resolution before the Vietnam War. Three months ago, President Bush did the same thing relative to Iraq. Senate Resolutions have been filed by Senators Byrd (#28) and Kennedy (#30) asking the President to come back to the Senate before committing troops in Iraq. Unfortunately, unless a Republican of stature, like Senator McCain of Arizona, joins this effort, the tide will continue in the wrong direction.

Second, no less than the Commandant of the Marine Corps has tried to warn the public that, this time, the casualties may be much greater than in the last Gulf War. If Saddam uses the chemical and biological weapons that we think he has, we will lose more than a few good men. More importantly, the Commanding Admiral for the Pacific has recently requested additional forces for Korean waters. Also, more forces are needed for the war on terrorism. A war on three fronts cannot be good military strategy.

Third, we have not exhausted our other options. For months, the French Government tried to tell us that we could quarantine this

Dictator, to put a "cordon sanitare" around him and leave him to stew in this own juice. It would take an American-lead coalition of Turks, Arabs, Syrians and Iranians plus a naval blockade, but it could be done.

Fourth, if we proceed, without the approval of the United Nations, to a "preemptive strike," we may well bring an end to that organization. It will go the way of the League of Nations and we shall return to a "Might makes Right" international jungle.

Wrong War Dangerous
to Home Defense

The military mind is notorious for fighting "the last war," when conducting a current war. We stand in danger of doing that now except it is the danger of conducting a conventional war or wars when confronted with a terrorist/gorilla type struggle. A piece by Benjamin and Simon entitled, "The Worst Defense," in the *New York Times* (2/20), points out that very little of the $160 billion in defense spending since 9/11 has been directed toward home defense. The "massive attack" theory probably will reduce casualties in our misguided war with Iraq, but it will do little toward bolstering defense here at home.

Since we seem comfortable in bed with the British these days, perhaps we should take a few pages out of their history. When confronted with the invasion of Britain by Napoleon, the Brits raised regiments of old and young men called, "Fencibles" to fight only within Britain, thus relieving their combat ready troops for the wars on the continent. They did the same thing in WWI and WWII except in those wars the term "Home Guard" was used. If that was a valid strategy (and it was) then bills introduced into the House by Charles Rangel (D-NY 15th) and Senator Hollings (D-SC) to revive the Draft make good sense. Defense Secretary Rumsfeld says these bills are not needed. They probably are not needed if the focus is on conventional warfare. However, who is going to patrol the pipelines, power lines, railroad tracks, bridges, reservoirs, atomic energy plants, pharmaceutical manufacturers, hospitals, monuments and shrines, etc. etc.? Viewed in that light, a counter bill by Ron Paul (R-TX 14th) to abolish the Selective Service looks like an extremely poor idea, indeed.

We had no choice in WWII but to fight on two fronts. That situation was forced on us by the geographic locations of our enemies. If we face many years, perhaps decades, of terrorist attacks, we had better be very careful how many foreign conflicts we take on. And, we had better make sure we have numerous allies in conducting these foreign operations.

Support Guards and Reservists

Politics do not end at the water's edge, but it sure as hell ends when your old Marine regiment has taken fire. Consider this: about half of our troops in Iraq are National Guard and Reservists. We could not fight a war like this without them. Further, if we stick to this "preemption strike" theory, we will be engaged in numerous other wars like this beyond Saddam. How then do we fight those many future wars?

Some say with a large standing army. That would certainly please the industrial-military complex that General Eisenhower said already had too much influence on the country. The drain on the budget would also make it impossible to do much in education and health. Anyway, Madison and Jefferson warned us against large standing armies and the danger such armies possessed for democracies. We ignore that warning at considerable risk.

Some say reintroducing the draft would do the job. However, the political party responsible for reintroducing the draft would probably wander in the wilderness for a long time. Also, our military leaders question whether a mandatory two-year or three-year required military service can provide us with the kinds of skilled manpower we need in today's highly sophisticated wars.

The better alternative seems to be a strong National Guard and Reserves. However, these citizen soldiers need help. After the Korean War, it proved difficult for several years to get enough Reservists and National Guards. In time, that shortage did ease. If our future is to be filled with many of these "on Presidential command" wars, that shortage will arise again.

We need stronger legislation on holding jobs for Guards and Reservists and on making up the difference in pay between their civilian jobs and their military jobs. We also need to extend and to strengthen educational benefits. In this area, some of the families of Reservist and Guard are suffering 50% reductions in income because they elected to serve their county. That is not right. Ask your national and state representatives to do more.

Good Wars/Bad Wars

Boots on the floor and body bags at the door. For the extreme patriot there is no bad war and for the pacifist there is no good war. The rest of us have to sort it all out.

Karl Von Clauswitz helps. This 19th Century writer believed that war was simply national self-interest, an extension of normal foreign policy. A less sympathetic interpretation might say war is greed. We have a lot of candidates for that category. Into it put all wars necessary to build the British, French, German, Spanish and Portuguese colonial empires. On our part, we can add the War of 1812, where we blatantly tried to steal Canada; the Mexican War; and the Spanish-American War. A hard-eyed view of the Gulf War might also allocate it to the bad category since oil played such an important role in the conflict.

Opposed to these are the good wars. It is easy to see where they differ from the first category. Greed plays a minor role here. These wars are fought for non-material goals. Central to their content and causality are matters of liberty, freedom, democracy, human rights and the like. The major revolutionary wars of the world: the English Civil War of the 17th Century, our own Revolutionary War, the French Revolution and the Russian Revolution belong clearly to this category. The American Civil War, both World Wars and the Korean War can also be found herein. Material gain was present in these wars, but it was not the major motivation.

Come now "Been Looney" and his ilk. For this man, who thinks he is Saladin the Magnificent, it is the 13th Century. He wishes to plunge us into another good war between the entire Muslim world and the rest of us. Religious nuts are bad for your health. There should be a Surgeon General's warning.

War is Hell,
But Madness May be Useful

General Sherman's famous phrase "War is Hell" may only tell a part of the story.

Just prior to the Texan War for Independence, an ancestor of mine, later to become Colonel Henry Karnes, was acting as a scout and was captured by Comanche Indians. The Scottish Karnes family tends to have reddish-brown hair, "ruagh" in the Gaelic. The Indians had never seen red hair. After taking Henry to the closest stream and unsuccessfully attempting to wash off what they thought must be a dye, they stood back perplexed. Henry "keened" (as the lowland Scots say) that the Indians might think him mad. So he began "to speak in tongues." It worked. Many tribes believe the mentally ill are "touched by the hand of the Great Spirit"; therefore, the Great Spirit also protects them. To harm them is to risk danger to oneself. So, they let him go "Scot free," as it were.

The second anecdote comes from World War II. This is the story of the mad piper of "D-Day." A Brigade commanded by Lord Lovat was in the attack wave at Omaha Beach and carried its usual section of pipers. Losses of pipers in World War I had been so high that, in World War II, Command discouraged using pipers in their traditional role, at the head of the advancing troops. But, Lovat thought otherwise. He ordered his piper (who is still living in Scotland) to sound the pipes. This he did, but to Lovat's amazement and admiration, he simply stood up in the midst of a hail of bullets and started marching back and forth in front of the lines. Oddly enough, he was not even shot at. When a captured German sniper was questioned after the landing, he was asked why he did not shoot such an obvious target. He replied, "The German Army does not shoot women, children, old men or priests. And we certainly do not shoot lunatics, either."

Leave it to the canny Scots to figure out that if war is going to be hell. Then, me lad, it's better off that you are to be the looniest coot in the bin.

The Corps: A Critical Assessment

The Marines have landed, this time in Afghanistan, and the situation is well in hand. Or is it? Winston Churchill once called the Soviet Union, "a riddle, wrapped in a mystery, surrounded by an enigma." He could have been speaking of the United States Marine Corps. That glamorous answer of the United States to the French Foreign Legion has been around since just before the Revolutionary War. We believe the record will show it is an organization capable of both great heroism, great stupidity and often the two combined.

For example, in World War II, the Battle of Tarawa should never have happened. One of the best Marine generals ever to serve, "Howling Mad" Smith, said of Tarawa, "Somebody should have been court-martialed for this." The Marines, if not the Navy, knew those coral reefs were too high for the Higgins boats. Australian intelligence had told them that, but they went in anyway, because Washington had to have a victory at that point in WWII and put intensive pressure on Admiral Halsey to get one. One Marine a minute died at Tarawa. One of the few Japanese survivors said, "We knew we were defeated because the U.S. Marines just kept on coming. No matter how many we killed, they just kept on coming."

Korea was no better. A monumental mistake put untrained reservists at the Chosen Reservoir to struggle with experienced Chinese troops. Men with no more than two summers of reserve training and only four weeks of combat training were sent with inadequate summer clothing to fight in 40 degree below zero weather. You're damn right: someone should have been court-martialed for that. On the other hand, the retreat to Hangnam was the most heroic military effort staged since Napoleon retreated from Moscow. Thank heavens the Chinese had no field artillery at their disposal and no air capability. If they had, an entire Marine Division would have been lost. That has never happened since the organization of the Corps. The Fourth Marine Regiment, the China Marines, burned their colors rather than surrender them to the Japanese in WWII. No Marine Divisional color has ever been struck anyplace to anyone.

The situation did not improve in Vietnam. It is very interesting to note that the Corps generally gets into trouble when it has to expand rapidly to meet some crisis. This probably points to a never corrected weakness in its reserve policy. Most people do not realize that more Marines were used in Vietnam than in World War II. That seems impossible, since six full divisions were activated for WWII. But Vietnam dragged on much longer than WWII, hence the need for more men. To be blunt about this: the mob that turned up in Marine Corps Recruit Depots in the 1960s drove many a drill instructor to reconsider his choice of vocation. Many recruits had drug addiction and serious delinquency problems before they ever reached the Corps. Again, as in Korea, there was not enough time to deal with those problems and they were much worse in Vietnam. Ultimately, of course, the Corps can be no stronger than the society from which it is recruited. American society had very serious problems in the 1960s.

When the flag went up on Mt. Surabachi, the Secretary of the Navy said the presence of that flag means a Marine Corps for another 200 years. Be thankful the man was right. In these days of small guerrilla actions and terrorist activities, the Corps is admirably designed to meet the challenge. Small, fast, rapidly mobilized, able to fight from sea-lift or sky-lift, capable of independent action without supply for months, it's the best larger elite military force we have going. When organized at its proper size, which is three full divisions and one division in reserve, it is larger than the Paratroopers, Rangers, Special Forces or Navy Seals, all of which are outstanding military units; however, none is designed to do the same thing the Marines do. Unfortunately, the Marines never do anything in understated manner. They don't dress that way. They don't act that way. When they foul up, you can depend upon it, they will foul up in a magnificent manner.

When you see that both grand and gaudy uniform coming down the street, know that it does not house a God, Goddess, or demigod. On occasion, it can house a hero or heroine. Mostly likely though, it is just the outer covering for men and women who make mistakes, correct those mistakes and then carry on. That is really why they are called, "a few good men."

This Time, No Tricks

This last Memorial Day left me with mixed emotions. I wanted very much to honor the men and women who saved Western Civilization in World War II and who are now leaving us in alarming numbers. The fact that their belated memorial in Washington D.C. has had to file for bankruptcy is a national shame. But I am also troubled by the many wars we have fought that could have been avoided.

Let's start with the War of 1812. The illegal search of ships on the high seas was the alleged cause of the war, but our attempt to steal what is now Canada was the real motive. We lost every major battle in that war, except the last one. The Black Watch stole the silver out of the White House; later, they gave it back. The war was so unpopular that the entire New England section of the country threatened to secede. Look at the Mexican War. An obscure Whig politician from Illinois named Abraham Lincoln stood on the floor of the House of Representatives and denounced that war. He said we tricked the Mexican government into hostilities. We did. "Remember the Maine." For what? We do not know to this day if it was a mine that sank the old battle ship or obsolete boilers.

"Ancient history," you say? Well, the Bay of Ton Kin is not ancient history. Congress gave the President the power to make that first step in an unsurpassed tragedy that cost this country over 37,000 in dead and missing, because one of our destroyers was allegedly attacked by North Vietnamese torpedo boats. A Naval board investigated the matter some time after the attack. A Naval aviator said this; "I was on patrol that night and had the best seat in the house. There were no enemy ships in the area. We were just firing into the darkness."

Korea is the right model. Wait for the call to come from the United Nations and then take action. If that call does not come, wait for overt aggression, as was true in the Gulf War, and then take action. Yes, it is absolutely true that we cannot appease dictators now, any more than we could in 1939. But let the threat be clearly proven. No more tricks.

Section V

"Congress shall make no law respecting an establishment of religion or prohibiting the free exercise thereof"

—First Amendment, U. S. Constitution

"The Constitution, a completely secular document, contains no references to God, Jesus or Christianity. It says absolutely nothing about the United States being officially Christian."

—Rob Boston, *Legacy of Freedom*, January 2003

V. Religion and Politics

A. Religion and Politics

B. Islam and Democracy

C. The "Morals" Controversy

D. In God We Trust?

Religion and Politics

The most explosive composition in this world is not to be found in dynamite. It is to be found in the combination of religion and politics. This dangerous mixture is so old that it is hard to know where to start to describe it. McCauley states it well in *Horatio at the Bridge*: "Then up spake brave Horatio the Captain of the Gate. To everyman upon this earth, death cometh soon or late. And how can man die better than facing fearful odds for the ashes of his father, and the temples of his Gods." Man has fought. For centuries and centuries he has fought. He has fought, defending his home, his family, his clan, his nation, and, yes, above all, his Gods.

It was in this spirit, that Nero and Julian tried to destroy Christianity, because they saw it as a mortal danger to the Roman Empire. Constantine, wiser than both, seeing that he could not beat the Christians, joined them. Whether he actually saw that cross in the sky and said, "In this sign, conquer," we will probably never know, but it saved the Roman Empire, at least for a time. In the 8th, 9th, and 10th Centuries, the Muslim horsemen carried jihad to the very gates of the European world with their shouts of "Death to the Infidel."

The Crusaders returned the compliment by killing every Muslim they could lay their hands on. When they could not find Muslims handy, they killed other Christians; for example, at Constantinople, Roman Catholics fought against Orthodox Catholics. In more modern times, the wars of the Reformation and Counter-Reformation laid waste to much of Europe. Cromwell massacred the Catholics at Drogheda. William of Orange devastated McCarthy on the banks of the Boyne, a fact that is remembered to this day in the Protestant marches in Northern Ireland. When Cromwell's army clashed with David Leslie's

Scots, both sides carried identical banners; they both read "God with us." That surely must have been confusing; if not to the contending parties, at least to the Deity.

During the "killing times" in the late 17th Century, Presbyterian ministers in Scotland preached with a pair of loaded pistols on the altar for fear the King's men might arrest them on sight. It is interesting how my good Presbyterian friends of today choose either to overlook this part of their church's history, or they just plain do not know it. In France, the Roman Catholic Church revoked the Edict of Nantes and then enlisted the aid of an increasingly out-of-touch Aristocracy to burn out the Protestant Huguenots. Then came the truly deplorable blood-bath of the French Revolution. The Church in France had unwisely sided with the Aristocracy and was nearly destroyed as a result of that alliance, just as the Church did many years later in Russia. Behind the holy icons of the Russian Orthodox Church, millions of Russian soldiers charged to their deaths in the wars of Tsarist expansion. We still live with the ramifications of that to this very day in Central Asia. What little credibility the Russian Church had was then destroyed in the Russian Revolution when the Church sided with the Whites against the Reds.

The unholy alliance of religion and politics continues to claim its victims. Muslims and Jews continue to kill each other in Palestine. Christians kill other Christians in Northern Ireland. Muslims and Christians kill each other in the Philippines. In Afghanistan, the "freedom fighters" enlisted Muslims throughout the world to fight against "Russian infidels." Not to be overlooked: when Osama Bin Laden sent his warriors against the World Trade Center, he did so with the injunction, "Kill the Crusaders." It matters not a whit that "jihad" can be interpreted as self-cleansing; that is, "war against the worst part of yourself." So it can; so it can. The finger of history writes and having writ moves on. Omar was dead right: you cannot take back a word of it.

The Founding Fathers, cognizant of much of this bloody and terrible history, deliberately and with considerable forethought, wrote the "establishment clause" into the American Constitution. Madison,

Jefferson via Madison, Franklin, and many others convened in Philadelphia, all knew what the deadly combination of religion and politics had done to this world. Now, it matters little that the actual words, "separation of church and state" do not appear in the Constitution. Somehow, in our concern over prayers in schools and mottoes on coins, we have missed what was obvious to the framers of the Constitution. They wanted to save us from the bloodshed of the past. So far, we have avoided the dreaded war of race against race. The slaughter of faith against faith must surely be an anathema to a benevolent God. The person who spoke the Sermon on the Mount could not have intended any of this. "Render unto Caesar what is Caesar's and unto God what is God's." If Jesus of Nazareth really spoke those words, perhaps he truly was the Messiah. At least, he will do, until a better one comes along.

Islam and Democracy

There are serious problems with Islam. No, it is not because they worship Allah and we worship God. Many see little difference between the two. Even the concept of "jihad" is not too troubling. Jihad can simply be interpreted as a continual struggle of good against evil. That is what most religions are about. However, one finds the term "Islamic Republic" to be close to an oxymoron. Moreover, the term "Islamic Democracy" may be a real oxymoron.

True, in recent year, there are forms of government that bill themselves as "Islamic Republics." The most well known is Iran. But, Iran is a theocracy in which representation is restricted to Muslims. Minorities such as Ba'hai and Zoroastrians have always been persecuted. Christians are not welcome, either. Certainly, no female has much representation in modern Iran. Remember, representation of women in both England and the United States was quite narrow until the middle of the 19th Century, so perhaps we should not throw stones.

We have yet to ascertain whether Democracy is compatible with Islam. There is nothing in history or in present governments to indicate that these are compatible concepts. Since the *Koran* is the supreme law of Islam, any constitution that is adopted in Muslim lands must conform to religious law as interpreted by the clerics. Thus, in Iran there is no concept of individual constitutional rights or limited government. A victory of the Shiite majority in Iraq might simply turn Iraq into another Iran. Further, if the goal of Iraqi organizations like Ansar al Islam is to restore the Caliphate, then no "infidels" have any rights including the right to live.

Two Wilsonian principles are in a head-on collision. We seek to make the world safe for Democracy, yet we uphold the right to self-determination. What do we do then, if Iraq in free elections chooses to adopt the same type of theocracy that Iran now has? Further, restoration of the Caliphate is simply not compatible with any Democracy anywhere.

The "Morals" Controversy

A recent Clarence Page commentary and recent letters by Illinois State University Professors Baker and Stewart in the *Pantagraph* have helped to clarify the discussion over politics and morals. Recent speeches by Robert Reich and Barack Obama have also helped. But, there is still a mystery here. Why is it that some voters object to positions on gay marriage and abortion while overlooking other matters that are just as morally suspect?

Is it morally wrong to vote tax cuts for the rich and not have enough public funds to aid the needy and the poor? Is it morally wrong to leave families without health insurance? Is it morally wrong to leave education starved for funds? Is it morally wrong to allow corporation executives to steal from their investors and their worker? Is it morally wrong to leave workers to "nickel and dime in America" without a living wage?

Is it morally wrong to damage the environment to increase corporate profits? Is it morally wrong to increase the profits of pharmaceutical companies while seniors cannot buy the medications they need? Is it morally wrong to weaken regulatory agencies to the point where one has safety considerations about the things one's children eat? Is it morally wrong to endanger workers' retirements by encouraging them to invest in fluctuating common stocks? Is it morally wrong to put the repayment of the national debt on the shoulders of one's children? Assuredly, it is morally wrong to wage an unnecessary war and kill over 200,000 Iraqis and 2,000 Americans.

Let's have one more just for Christmas. Is it morally wrong to outsource jobs so that parents cannot provide clothes and toys for their children? This is doubly morally wrong since it is also wrong to buy toys and clothing made in sweatshops in Asia, which employ children in unhealthy conditions.

I do not claim to be learned in religious matters. Someone is going to have to carefully explain to me how ANY of the above items can be consistent with the Sermon on the Mount given by Jesus of Nazareth.

In God We Trust?

We appear to be having trouble with our old motto: "In God we trust." Would it help any to think in terms of "In the works of God we trust"? Surely we can agree on some good works. For me, the hand of God was present in the Constitutional Convention when the founders tried hard for "a more perfect union." It was present also in the Bill of Rights. Unfortunately, what we could not get done with the pen in the 18th Century, we had to finish with the bayonet in the Civil War. It was present in the struggles of the Abolitionists and in the life of Lincoln. I find it in the speeches and life of Martin Luther King, Jr. I can see it in the words of Franklin Roosevelt, "We have nothing to fear but fear itself." I can even see it in the lives of Lyndon Johnson and Jack Kennedy, imperfect men beyond a doubt, but men dedicated to making life better for the average person.

If you do not like looking for the hand of God in mere men, then try looking at events, particularly in WWII. There was no good reason for the United States' achieving the atom bomb before Nazi Germany. The German scientists were ahead in that race before the irrational actions of a mad man, Adolph Hitler, put them behind. Logically, the Brits should not have been able to get off that beach at Dunkirk. Do you want to ascribe it to chance alone that our dive-bombers happened to get through at Midway, when our torpedo planes were wiped out completely? How about Pearl Harbor? Was it just chance that every aircraft carrier we had was not in port when the Japanese struck?

Perhaps the Zoroastrians had it right, long before the Jews and the Christians. There is a force for good in this world. They called it Ahura Mazda, the God of Light, and it made itself known through the presence of the Sun. Somehow, someplace we stuck a sign up in the window that says, "Only the Judo-Christian God need apply." We are beyond that.

Section VI

"Doublespeak: words 'deliberately constructed for political purposes: words, that is to say, which not only had in every case a political implication, but were intended to impose a desirable mental attitude upon the person using them.'"

—George Orwell's lexicography

VI. The Bush Administration

Mickey for President

The current administration's record is so bad that the Democrats could run Mickey Mouse and stand a good chance of winning. The Bush Administration's failed foreign policy ranks with that of JFK's, LBJ's and Jimmy Carter's. As Senator Byrd points out in his recent book, *Losing America*, the Congress has surrendered the power to make war to the Executive Branch. As a result, we are in another quagmire like Vietnam. We have the pathetic image of a President, having turned his back on the United Nations, now having to go from foreign capital to foreign capital begging for support to keep the peace in Iraq, Afghanistan, the Philippines, perhaps Liberia and Sudan, and God knows where else. The only countries lining up to help us do that, with the exception of Britain, are poor countries hoping for a possible hand out.

The Bush policy of "preemptive strike" depends on accurate military intelligence, which we certainly do not possess. If we did, where were the weapons of mass destruction? Where is Osama? How much nuclear progress has Iran made? What kind of nuclear power does North Korea possess? Many believe such a policy was immoral in the first place—a retreat to "might makes right." The war in Iraq was not even an unqualified military success. It came close to being that in the early phases, but this administration then blindly forgot to plan for the occupation. There can only be one overall conclusion. The Bush foreign policy has been illegal, immoral and inefficient from the beginning.

The Bush internal economic policies are not much better. We have a report from the Economic Policy Institute showing that the change in unemployment in the first two years of the Bush administration is worse than at any time since the administration of Herbert Hoover. We also have a petition from over eighty economists, including eleven Nobel Prize winners, stating their opinion that the tax cuts are irresponsible, will put us further in hock, and will not stimulate the economy. We have studies indicating that the inequality of wealth in this country is now greater than it was in England between the world wars.

The regulatory agencies, including the Securities and Exchange Commission, have been weakened. This at a time when we have flagrant corporate thievery, as in Enron and Halliburton, that is worse than at any time since the McKinley Administration. The environmental policy is in shreds.

We have Reservists refusing to go back to Iraq after serving their initial hitch. A selective service draft may be just around the corner since an all-volunteer Army cannot handle multiple wars all around the globe. Ah, Nuts! Bring on the ears! I'm voting for Mickey

Compromise Again

In a recent letter in the *Pantagraph*, Phil Buffington asks for an example of compromise from the liberal side of the aisle. I am happy to respond.

Conservatives believe in de-centralization of governmental functions. Rather than provide all the tax reductions the Bush Administration has in mind, suppose we take some of that money and send it to state governments in the form of revenue sharing. We could either earmark these new federal funds for education and health, or we could leave it to the discretion of hard-pressed state governments as to where they could best use these funds.

In recent years, one of the largest state government burdens has been in the area of Medicaid. Just relieving the Medicaid costs alone would help greatly with the present difficult budget situation in Illinois. Three decades ago, we had federal revenue sharing, which most states, including Illinois, used for educational costs. In 1973, we needed roughly $300 million to fund a major change in the school finance system. It is true that a part of the costs of that reform came from new state taxes, but a part also came from federal revenue sharing.

Federal revenue sharing can have a domino effect. Funds made available through the federal government can dislodge state money, which can be used at the local level. The "compromise" comes when we have to strike some agreement about shifting the level at which government services take place, versus downsizing all government services. We can make administrative cost savings through shifting functions from the nation to the state to the locality. But, you cannot expect, and should not expect the liberal side to agree to large reductions in these services. It will not work AT ALL for the federal government to merely require more services at the state and local levels and then not provide funding for those services. All of this is not new. Senator Adlai Stevenson introduced several bills to accomplish this in the 1970s; there had been earlier bills of this nature in the House. Stop reinventing the wheel. Read some history.

Does President Bush Have a Mandate?

President Bush claims he has a mandate to continue his foreign policy and his domestic policies for the next four years with a popular vote of 51%. Does history support his claim? Only partially. If we take the percentage of the popular vote as an indicator of "mandate" we get this record. Presidents who got more than 60% of the popular vote might well believe they had a mandate. Only four Presidents since the Civil War attained that kind of popular support: Richard Nixon in 1972, Lyndon Johnson in 1964, Franklin Roosevelt in 1936, and Warren Harding in 1920. If we lower the cut to 58% of the popular vote we can add: Ronald Reagan, Dwight Eisenhower, and Herbert Hoover. In the middle of the Civil War, Abraham Lincoln could obtain only 55% of the popular vote.

Winning margins vary through history. From the Civil War to the end of the 19th Century, margins were relatively small. Through the first half of the 20th Century, they grew. In the last half of the 20th Century, they again became small. It would be interesting to make some international comparisons here. In a large and heterogeneous republic such as ours, smaller margins may well be the expectation and only wars, depressions, etc. may produce the larger wins.

George W. does join a list of only thirteen Presidents, since the McKinley Administration, to be a majority President. Ronald Reagan received a majority twice, as did Eisenhower. Franklin Roosevelt received a majority all four times he ran for the office. This list favors the

Republicans since ten of the majority Presidents were Republicans, while only three were Democrats.

There are other more detailed ways to measure a "mandate" such as the margin in the House and the Senate that were elected at the same time as the Presidential candidate. On gains of seats by an incumbent President "W's" case looks best. Only Bush Junior and Franklin Roosevelt gained seats for their party while being re-elected. However, it is still stretching the term to call President Bush's recent election victory a mandate. "Preference" is certainly defensible, but not a mandate.

In any event, we get a chance to test President Bush's "mandate" claim in less than two years. If his party increases their seats in House and Senate in the "off year" of 2006, the mandate claim would look a lot stronger. Of course, "W" would have only two more years left to serve in his constitutionally-limited eight-year span. The last two years of any "Lame Duck" president could never be as strong as the period preceding that last two years. So, as in too many matters these days, the Spin Doctors do their thing and few citizens go back and actually check out their claims. Taken far enough, perhaps the Nazi propagandists were correct: if you tell the people enough times that is it true and they will eventually come to believe that it is true, whether it actually is or not. Perhaps all political literature should be understood to wear the label, "Let the Buyer Beware."

Bad Public Policy

The proposal to privatize social security is bad public policy. In the first place, it rests on another phony crisis, just like the WMDs in Iraq. There will not be a shortfall of funds until about 2040. George F. Will virtually admits this in his commentary in the *Pantagraph* of January 20th. This shortfall could easily be made up by rescinding the tax cuts given to the rich by this administration and placing those funds into the social security trust fund. Such a bill has been proposed by Representative Obey of Wisconsin.

Second, allowing this privatization will require a reduction in the amounts now provided to social security beneficiaries unless the federal government borrows about two trillion dollars to make up for money which will be going into private accounts. This further increase in the national debt will cause the dollar to continue its downward side, which, in turn at some point, must cause a rise in the interest rates in the USA.

Third, investing in stocks is always subject to fluctuations in the market. On a long bear market, individual investments might well be so depleted there would be little left to maintain a decent retirement. If investing in stocks is such a good idea, then let the social security trust fund do it so the risk will be spread equally to all clients.

Fourth, unless capped, deposits in individual retirement accounts will be much easier for the wealthy to make than for the poor. This will fuel income and wealth inequalities in the United States, which are already the greatest among the developed nations of the world.

Fifth, this will be a bonanza for stockbrokers, banks and other Wall Street types, which are already the most favored citizens under the Bush administration.

Why do such a thing? Because it fits the rigid ideological stance of the Bushites, which G. F. Will partially shares. Make no mistake, the real goal here is NOT to "reform" social security; it is to eliminate social security, then Medicare, then minimum wage, etc.

Old Europe?

[Editorial Note: For a darker picture of Europe, see David Brooks, "Fear and Rejection," *New York Times*, June 2, 2005.]

The spectacular collapse of the dollar relative to the Euro has not yet brought on the return to high interest rates in the U.S. economy. We can probably thank the Chinese, the Japanese and the Saudis for that. After all, the Chinese want to continue selling us most of our clothing. The Japanese want somewhere to invest other than in their own shaky banks. The Saudis want to continue selling us oil. So, all three continue to show up to buy the U.S. government's debt, of which we now have lots and lots, thanks to the very unsound economic policies of the Bush Administration. The day will come, however, when all three will not want to put their money into a falling currency. Then, you can watch your mortgage and your credit card rates go through the ceiling.

In the meantime, the European Union (EU) has been outscoring the United States in some other areas. Many of these are documented in Jeremy Rifkin's *The European Dream*. Presently, income inequalities are much greater in the United States than in Europe. Of the developed nations in the world, only Russia and Mexico have greater income inequality than the USA. Our overall productivity as measured by the Gross Domestic Product (GDP) has fallen behind the European Union, $10.5 trillion to $10.4 trillion. If we subtract defense spending out of that, the EU leads us now by $10.50 trillion to $10.16 trillion. Europe now boasts 2.6 million millionaires, while North America has only 2.4 million, despite the best efforts of the Bush Administration to assist the rich.

Every index is not economic. What about the fact that the European Union has 322 physicians per 100,000 people, while the USA has only

279; and that the average life expectancy is 78.2 years in the EU compared to 76.9 years in the United States? The average vacation time across Europe is six weeks which is mandated by national laws, causing Europeans to say that Europeans "work to live," while Americans "live to work." You really do not want to hear about European to American education comparisons, do you?

Donald Rumsfeld calls this the "Old Europe." I don't think so.

Section VII

"Lives of great men all remind us, we can make our lives sublime and departing leave behind us footprints in the sands of time."

—Henry Wadsworth Longfellow

VII. Testimonials

A. Another Voice of Reason is Silenced

B. Paul Simon's Unfinished Agenda

C. Tallest Tree in the Forest

D. A Different Kind of Dear John Letter

E. A Tribute to Ben Hubbard

F. Wabash on My Little Mind

G. Undervalued

H. My Charlie

Another Voice of Reason is Silenced

By Benjamin C. Hubbard

Distinguished Professor Emeritus, Illinois State University

In the cacophony of shrill partisan political debate, we can ill afford to lose the few voices of calm reasoning we have left. Together with my colleague, Alan Hickrod, I had the privilege and honor of working with Paul Simon when he was serving in the Illinois legislature, when he was Lt. Governor, and when he was a United States Senator. There was no one who was more willing to put aside partisan affiliation and work for the common good than Paul Simon.

On many occasions, I have walked into his office to be greeted by this kind of question, "Ben, who is really interested in this bill and why are they interested in it?" Since Hickrod and I were representing, not organized educational interests in the state, but only what we believed to be good educational policy, Paul knew that we had very little by way of funds to contribute to his many campaigns. That did not stop him from giving us more time than we probably deserved. His door was always open to good ideas, even if you didn't have a dime.

In those days, Democrats were a permanent minority party in McLean County, so he would call ahead and ask if there were enough Democrats to have a decent meeting. It was his way of making sure that minority interests were well represented. It is difficult to imagine what his frustration level would be if he were still sitting in the present US Senate, which pays less and less attention to minority interests.

Finally, a word about his well-known fiscal conservatism. Although he always insisted on quality for dollar spent, there was never a day that he did not support both spending and taxes if he thought them necessary for the public welfare. I remember vividly one day in Chicago when the door to a meeting burst open and reporters swarmed out yelling, "We've got him. We've got him. He said he would raise taxes." I asked him what he did. He said, "I told the people the truth." The loss of that kind of statesman is a monumental disaster.

Paul Simon's Unfinished Agenda

The late Paul Simon left many a legacy to the citizens of Illinois. Within that legacy are two small books published in the last year of his life, *Healing America* and *Our Culture of Pandering*. Both contain a list of public policy recommendations that he would have supported had he continued among us.

The problem is that in our world of sound bites and quick fixes, not enough people will sit down and read even this total of approximately 340 pages. So, I tried to summarize some of his recommendations. There is a danger in such a summarization, because I may have emphasized the wrong points or given a twist to the recommendations that Paul would not have approved. If I have, then there is a quick remedy, just read the little volumes yourself.

First and foremost, the late Senator would have wished to repeal much of the Bush tax cuts and use at least a part of those funds to pay down the towering national debt. All of his life, Paul was an advocate of "pay as you go" government. We have all heard him repeat, almost as a mantra, "If you don't want to tax for the public services, then do without the public services." Fighting a war "on the cuff" would be the very last thing he would support.

He deplored the increasing interest on the national debt for many reasons. In the first place, those are funds that, for the most part, go to rich people, thereby constituting a transfer of funds from the poor to the rich. They also constitute a flow of funds outside the United States to foreign creditors of this government. Also, the ever-increasing national debt contributes to the slide in the value of the dollar. The fact that the dollar has lost a quarter of its value relative to the Euro in the last eighteen months would have sent him literally through the roof. "Tax cuts are good for you and me," he said, "but they are not good for our children and grandchildren. They are good politics but bad economics."

As might be expected, this son of a Lutheran minister and brother of a Lutheran minister did not support the war in Iraq. He felt it could have been avoided. However, he would have supported the rebuilding of Iraq. He constantly felt that we did not do enough in foreign aid. There was hardly a speech that he gave in which he did not point out that foreign aid constitutes less than one half of one percent of the federal budget and that we were last among the rich nations of the world in the percentage of our budget that we give to foreign aid. One cannot be sure what he would make of the current Bush immigration proposals, but we can be sure that he felt immigration strengthened, not weakened, this country.

The Senator believed very strongly in education and wished to raise support for college students to at least half of what it was under the G.I. Bill of Rights. In secondary education, he would have supported increasing federal aid to the states in order to reduce the gap between the poor school districts and the rich school districts within those states. He deplored the lack of emphasis on foreign languages in American schools and doubtless would have supported federal aid in that area, as well. He would have strongly supported education in our prison systems. The fact that we have four percent of the population of the world and 25 percent of its prisoners was deeply troubling to him. The reform of the prison system would have been high on his unfinished agenda.

The Senator strongly supported campaign finance legislation and was especially concerned with the effect of payments of special interests upon legislation. He found the fact appalling that the British run their entire national election on the amount that one candidate spent to run for Mayor of New York City. He was not a supporter of gambling as a source of funds for public purposes. Much of this opposition stemmed from the use of gambling contributions to candidates' campaign coffers.

Paul Simon was a Democrat, but he strongly believed in a republican form of government and not in a direct democracy. He was especially scornful of those who slavishly follow the latest opinion poll. He pointed out that the reason political parties seem so similar comes largely from the fact that the polls are telling the same thing to both sides of the aisle. As the title of one of his books indicates, he was opposed to pandering in politics and in any other aspect of life, especially in the media. Above the editorial page editors' desk in too many newspapers, said Paul, was the motto, "Don't offend the public. Don't offend the advertisers. Don't be too controversial." "Editorials," he concluded, "need more backbone and muscle." Newspaper mergers do not provide a good climate for that, so he introduced unsuccessful legislation that would limit those consolidations.

Finally, the Senator urged far more participation in politics than we currently have. One can almost see him pointing his finger at a citizen and saying, "And who gave you permission to sit on the sidelines?"

Tallest Tree in the Forest

If your ear was pointed toward Chicago, last week, you doubtlessly heard the lightning strike the tallest tree in the forest. When a stroke caught up with Senator John Maitland, it felled one of the last remaining strong supporters of public education in this state. While we do not know the extent of the stroke's damage, it cannot be good for education. John Maitland belonged to, indeed led, that rare group of Republicans who put funding for education in a special category, outside other public spending.

There is literature on the subject. It is referred to as the "doctrine of unique function" and holds that spending on education is not like other public spending in that it is more investment than it is consumption. The late Senator from Ohio, Robert Taft, led this group nationally at one time. With the death of Charles Claybough and the retirement of Gene Hoffman, its numbers have declined in the Illinois General Assembly. The retirement of Maitland's counterpart on the Democratic side, Senator Arthur Berman, does not help matters either. The number of "unique function" men has thinned in the halls of academe as well. We just cannot afford to find former Marine John Maitland on the casualty list.

A Different Kind of Dear John Letter

Mr. Penn, the McLean County Democratic Chairperson, and Mr. Wilson, the self-appointed spokesperson for the Republican Right, have sent their "Dear John letters" to Senator Maitland. We are sending here a different kind of letter to the ailing Senator. John, by your exemplary service you have earned the right to at least a full year's recovery from your stroke, perhaps more. You have fought many a battle for just causes. Fight this one now for all of the men and women who have struggled, or who are struggling, to come back from serious medical problems. You now represent a special constituency, the recovering, who are found on both sides of the political aisle. Does Mr. Parrott, the McLean County Republican Chairman, really believe it will be easy to find another man or woman who has so well represented both moderate Republicans and moderate Democrats? Does he really want to set off a war between the right and the middle within his own party? We think not to both questions.

A Tribute to Ben Hubbard

Ben C. Hubbard grew up in one of the poorest counties of Alabama. His father was a country preacher and his mother was a schoolteacher. The ancient Tribunes of Rome were called "men of the people" and so, assuredly, was Ben Hubbard. He was a Liberal Democrat all of his life, but he lived in an age in which this country was not so rigidly divided by political ideologies. If anything, he was consulted on school finance matters more in Illinois when Republicans were in a majority than when Democrats were in a majority. He was the "guru," trusted implicitly by both sides of the aisle. Noted professors of school finance of the past have also played that role: William McLure, Paul Mort, Roe L. Johns, all come to mind. At the time all these men were active, perhaps school finance could be separated from partisan politics. That is still not a bad strategy, but it seems much more difficult to do that in recent years.

I will limit my remarks here to Ben's spectacular performance with the General Assembly of Illinois through more than three decades. While he tried to steer clear of partisan politics; nevertheless, he knew the practical and regional politics of school finance better than any man alive. He was to that field what Michael Jordan was to basketball. There are none better to speak on this subject than I, because I was privileged to struggle at his side for public education in Illinois during most of those three decades.

Many have said that to be a skilled politician you must first learn to count. Ben Hubbard did that very well. He knew from his first day in Illinois that there was no way on earth to get what he wanted through the Illinois legislature from only the votes on the Democratic side of the aisle. Ben was a life-long Democrat, but he assiduously, and with great patience, cultivated a group of votes on the Republican side of the aisle that he could usually count on when push came to shove. In my judgment, Ben Hubbard was the most effective lobbyist public education ever had in this state.

His legislative successes are even more remarkable when you understand that his major goal in life was to increase the opportunities of poor kids in poor districts. To do that, he had to fine-tune the financial structure in order to send state money to those districts that were most in need. That meant sending money not only to poor districts, but also to poor students in the more wealthy districts. This was not a hidden agenda; Ben was very open about it. If the wealthy suburbs had been following only their pocketbook interests, they should have opposed him completely. Sometimes they did, but not all of the time. Why?

First, through his work with the former Illinois School Problems Commission, this man was accepted as "the expert" on school finance. When he took a policy position, he had the facts to back up that position. Ben did not really like to argue political or educational ideology. He tried to get down to basic data just as soon as he could.

Second, he didn't speak like a university professor. Never in his whole life, did he talk down to a member of the Legislature—never. He had run for public office back in Bibb County, Alabama, and genuinely liked and admired the politicians in the General Assembly. And, they liked him. Also, it was well known that Ben came from a poor background. He had a way of making rich folks feel guilty, yes guilty, without making them feel mad. This is a very powerful technique that others have used, not the least of which was Delite Morris at the university level in Illinois. Ben was also a master of building the necessary compromises needed to pass legislation. More than any man I ever saw, he could "put a gift on the Christmas tree for everybody and then figure out the wiring later." I have tried that little trick and my trees generally blew up in my face.

Assuredly, his strengths were also his weaknesses. When he made his move for the state superintendency, he had just a little too much of the "common touch." He was deliberately discriminated against. Because he spoke with a Southern accent, he could not be totally trusted by Northern Liberals, some of whom were African-American. What a travesty of justice! What an absolute travesty! No man or woman who ever held an appointment at Illinois State University did more for African-Americans than he did. But, none of us escapes the dead hand of our past. He suffered the fate of a number of other white Southern Liberals at the state and national levels.

I really don't think he was appreciated as much at Illinois State University as he should have been, except when ISU almost lost its lab school and he saved it. I remember his walking into my office on the day after he pulled that off and said, "Alan, last night, I used up every legislative chip I had; we probably will not be able to pass another piece of school finance legislation for at least a decade." He was almost right. I feel that even his fellow faculty members in the College of Education did not appreciate the fact that he spent endless hours in Springfield and then got up and came to work at the same time as all the rest of the faculty did. Committee meetings in Springfield often ended at midnight or one o'clock in the morning. Then came that long two-hour drive back to Bloomington. He drove; I slept. This went on for decades. He arranged for my classes to meet later in the day or in the evening because he knew I would probably not stand up to that grind. He never ever made things easy for himself.

So, let us salute the Tribune of the People from Bibb County. Your cause continues; the battle rages; the bugles still call forth good men to strive for the right. Today, the ranks of those who fought with you are thinning; the Old Guard stands not to muster; and the memories of past struggles will soon be lost. But, no soldier ever carried the flag of equal educational opportunity in Illinois further than you, Colonel Hubbard. None ever will.

Wabash on My Little Mind

Fifty years is a very long time, but here goes. The year is 1948. A group of very scared freshmen is huddled in a study group in Kane House. They are certain they will flunk Dean Byron Trippet's Western Civilization course. Trippet had a reputation of being a tough grader. It is a group of six or eight, but memory allows me to recall only Andy Andrews, Don Cole, Gene Reeves, Bill Reinke and myself. For some unknown reason, I got the task of coordinating this group. I must have done a halfway decent job, because we all passed the course. Thanks, Gents, because right then and there, I got the crazy idea that I might someday make a reasonably good college professor; and I did. I don't think my freshman roommate, the late Whitey Telligman, was in that study group. Perhaps he was not in Trippet's course at the time. Whitey was a strong silent type; so, later, I was not surprised to find that he had joined the Marine Corps. I can't square my memory of him with his also being a banker, which he later became, in California.

Professors do have an influence on all of us. For me they were: Byron Trippet, Jack Charles, and Bob Harvey. Trippet was important to me several times. First, in my sophomore year, my grades began to slip because my old friend Thomas Jefferson Lee and I started making a few too many trips to Danville for various and sundry pleasures that I do not care to detail in a public document. The Dean called me in and I got the standard Gentleman's Code lecture but with a twist. Byron Trippet came from Princeton, Indiana, and he knew my family in Fort Branch, Indiana. The towns are only a few miles apart. Our little chat must have been effective because I did a little better the second semester. I think I knew he was fully capable of calling my Dad, for a little man-to-man discussion about his son's wayward activities. The "Gentleman's Code" did allow for family influence.

Bob Harvey, on the other hand, simply scared the living hell out of me. I had been a pretty big frog in a very little pond in Fort Branch High School (valedictorian, president of the senior class and all the rest). The first two papers I got back from Bob Harvey were straight out "F." Me, the valedictorian, given an "F." I kept those papers in my drawer all the years that I was at Wabash. The night they inducted me into Phi Beta Kappa, I took them out, looked up and said, "Thank you, Bob, with all my heart."

John Frederick Charles, Lafayette Professor of Greek and Latin, was the third professor with a profound influence on me. Coming from a little rural town in Indiana, he was the first, living, breathing, real scholar I had ever seen. He once said, "I suppose you might say that I am kept alive by books." I know now that's a variation on one of Jefferson's similar statements, but I sure as hell did not know that then. Often, in my own retirement, I have thought of another one of his observations about his retirement: "There are many things I should do, but nothing that I must do." He taught me ancient history, medieval history, Latin and French. But most importantly, he taught me that the son of an automobile dealer and grandson of a farmer could be a scholar, too. Many years later, when I walked across that stage at Harvard with a doctorate in my hand, you better believe I thought of "the owl of Athens." I think I was the only member of our class at his funeral.

In the fall of 1950, T.J. Lee was standing on the porch of the house in which we lived holding a large letter. His face was about as sad as I ever recall its being. It was an order from the Commandant, United States Marine Corp, to Private G. Alan Hickrod to report for active duty. T.J. had lost his leg at the Battle of the Bulge. He knew war. I took the letter and went over out of respect to Dean Trippet, thinking we would spend only a few minutes on formalities. He asked his secretary to hold his appointments. For an hour or so we walked around the yard talking. Most of it was about his service in the Second World War, but he made me solemnly promise that if I survived, I would come back to Wabash and finish what I had started. I promised him that and I did it. There is a brick over there in the walk that says simply, "To the memory of Byron Trippet." You need not ask who put it there.

In my senior year, we talked a third time. I was a pretty serious student by then, except for an occasional lapse in the Beta Theta Pi house, where a former Sergeant in the Marine Corps seemed always a welcome guest though he was never a member. I hit the books rather hard. Dean Trippet wanted me to apply to Harvard but I didn't think I had it in me to do that. Finally, he convinced me to apply to a Master of Arts in Teaching program in their Graduate School of Education with the argument that I could always find my way into secondary education, if some college or university doors did not open up. I had the good sense to listen to him. Charlie Finch, another Wabash man, and I went off together to Cambridge, Massachusetts—but that's another story. In the thirty-one years that I was a university professor I taught over two thousand students, both undergraduate and graduate. I directed over one hundred doctoral dissertations. To the very best of my ability, I passed on everything that Wabash gave me to those students. Yes, the Gentleman's Code and all.

It's a long way from the lonely sound of a coalmine whistle in southern Indiana to the cheerful sound of the chapel bells in the Harvard Yard. Thank you, gentlemen, for that trip. I owe you all more than I can ever repay.

Undervalued

On the last Ides of March, the *Manchester Guardian*, a world-class newspaper, carried a quarter page obituary headed, "A Gifted and Intelligent Master of the Dance Dies." It duly recorded this man's service in British Intelligence and in the Foreign Service. It also traced his career from Ballet Rambert through Sadler's Wells to the Transvaal Ballet and to Covent Garden. Also noted was his establishment of American-Scottish ballet, which regularly performed at the Edinburgh Festival Fringe.

This man's name was Alexander Bennett. That's right. The same man who headed ballet activities in Bloomington-Normal for over a decade. The same man who, after all those years of faithful service to this community, was summarily dismissed without an adequate notice. If Alex had been a little less trustful and had consulted a lawyer before signing his last contract, certain folk might still be paying through their noses for his shabby treatment.

The greatest damage, though, was to the art he loved so much. Ballet does not have strong roots in Bloomington-Normal. The poor treatment of Alex did nothing to make it grow. Worse yet, this is not an isolated incident. Our record for supporting "the best" is not at all good in the Twin Cities. We have let excellent restaurants close time and time again because of low patronage. Le Petite Bistro's closing is the most recent example of this. There are other examples in retail sales, as well. If this were a poor community, it might be argued that we cannot afford such "frills" in life. But that is not true. Normal has one of the higher incomes in the state and the area has a very low 2.5% unemployment. No, the answer I am afraid, is that we have simply not learned an important lesson: society benefits little by cultivating mediocrity.

My Charlie

Charlie Finch and I went to Cambridge, MA, to the Harvard Graduate School of Education in 1954. Charlie had just returned from a tour of duty in Japan; I had finished Wabash College, after a tour of duty in the United States Marine Corps. I have a lot of pleasant memories of those years.

Because of his service in Japan, some of the Japanese graduate students living in the same dorm with us talked often to Charlie. On one occasion, Charlie broke out his home movies of Tokyo and invited the Japanese students to view them. Things were rolling along rather well until the picture of US Occupation Headquarters surrounded by a large metal fence came on the screen. Then, from the back of the room came an angry growl, and very clearly the words were shouted, "NATIONAL SHAME." Without saying a word, Charlie hit the fast forward button. The next thing he said was, "And here are the beautiful gardens in the park." Charlie was not always a diplomat, but he could be one if needed.

On another occasion, the Japanese students invited us to a saki party. I suspect that I had a slight advantage here, because in the Corps we consumed a good deal more of John Barleycorn than did an occupation Army. However, I was well on my way to not knowing which one of the Hickrod boys I was; Charlie was in no better condition. He got up unevenly, went to the door, looked down the hall, and then motioned for me to come outside the room. I did. He said, "Look there." The Japanese graduate students were leaving the party, taking a cold shower, and returning to the party for more libations. No wonder we could not keep up.

Much later in life, when Charlie had assumed duties at Wabash College, he would stop and stay overnight with me, either going to or coming from Crawfordsville. I looked forward to those stops a lot because Charlie was always well read and usually had just finished a book he wanted to talk about. Charlie was primarily a Liberal Democrat, as am I. So our conversations often turned on how disappointed both of us were with the first Bush Administration. Later, our conversations inevitably focused on the Iraq war.

As Mister Finch, Charlie had one set of reasons for opposing the war, but as Colonel Finch he had a different set of reasons for opposing the war. As a civilian, he thought the war could have been avoided, as did a number of us. Colonel Finch, however, had special qualifications for evaluating this military effort. In the late 1970s, Charlie had helped write the field manuals for the US Army Civil Affairs units and spent sixteen years in that Army specialization. He still had access to these field manuals on-line. As news of the rioting and the looting of the Baghdad National Museum filtered back to this country, he knew immediately that something had gone terribly wrong. Eventually, he discovered that, when the Army invaded Iraq, it had less than 400 men in civil affairs units and the Marine Corps had absolutely none at all.

The Civil Affairs units, which were mostly reserve units, not regular units, had not been mobilized because the directors of this war had felt they would not be needed. The Cheney, Rumsfeld, Wolfowitz, Rice, etc. group thought we would be greeted with thrown flowers and the sound of brass bands. What was thrown was fire from AK-47s and shoulder held rockets. The sounds heard were not from bands, but from suicide car bombs. Since there was not supposed to be an occupation in the first place, the men and women that know how to conduct an occupation successfully (the Civil Affairs units) were simply not there to do the job. Charlie tried to bring this very serious mistake to the attention of the Post Dispatch in St. Louis, but I don't think they did much with it.

I suppose there is no such thing as a silver lining in a death. However, I cannot help but suspect that it is a good thing that Colonel Finch no longer has to worry about the incompetent people who are conducting the Iraq war. Sometimes, when I get tired of opposing this absolute idiocy (and I surely do), I can almost hear Charlie saying, "Stay with it, Alan, if only for my sake." I will, Charlie, I will.

Section VIII

"Some books are to be tasted, others to be swallowed, and some few to be chewed and digested."

—Francis Bacon

VIII. Book Reviews

An Academic Life on the Prairie

Professor Emeritus Earl A. Reitan of Normal continues his autobiography with *Time Is/Time Was/Time Nevermore Shall Be*, a sequel to his earlier published *Crossing the Bridge*, which described his youth in a Norwegian-American culture. This new volume takes him through the balance of his life, including the many years he taught at Illinois State Normal University and then at Illinois State University and finally into retirement.

The book is of interest on several levels. First, for students of the sociology of education who wish to add flesh and bones to the dry statistical evidence of education used as upward mobility, this is quite a find. This man pulled himself up by his own bootstraps from the dull, boring backwater of small towns in Minnesota and the Dakotas to the Reading Room of the British Museum in London. I know how far that is since I made a similar trip from a small coal-mining town in southern Indiana to the halls of Harvard. Every good autobiography should be entitled *X and His Times*. If you want to understand the Great Depression read about what it did to the Reitan family in the upper Midwest.

Second, students of the administration of higher education will find it interesting because it gives an honest appraisal of what life was like at Illinois State University in the 1950s, 1960s and 1970s. This is no white wash job. ISU has always had an academic inferiority complex. If you want to see what the source of this complex is you should read Reitan's book. At a time when Northern Illinois University was making great strides toward becoming a multipurpose institution, Illinois State was held back. Reitan does not assign blame for this. As far as this reviewer is concerned the buck always stops at the President's desk.

Finally (this is a little unusual), there is more than a touch of intellectual history here. Reitan tells you what he was reading, what books he was writing and why he was writing them. He tells you of his long interest in the role of the "public intellectual," the person who is supposed to influence the actual decision makers. A role he, himself, has filled in another of his books entitled, *Liberalism*, a book intended for the general reader, as is his autobiography. Professor Reitan has written many books aimed at an academic audience. His publication in 2001, *The Thatcher Revolution,* was especially well received in those circles. It is to be hoped that he will return to the "public intellectual stance" in the near future.

[*Time Is/Time Was/Time Nevermore Shall Be*, can be found at Babbitt's Books, 104 North St., Normal, Illinois, (309-454-7303) for $19.95]

The Kaleidoscopic Hillary

Probably, no book in recent years has been reviewed as many times as Simon and Schuster's *Living History* by Senator Hillary Rodham Clinton. Each reader and reviewer will see a different facet of this remarkable lady. She is politician, lawyer, diplomat, mother, wife and woman. From her earliest days as a Goldwater Girl, she has been immersed in a political milieu. She began on the Republican side. Not until the McGovern campaign, did she take a position as a Democrat. It must be a tribute to her very persuasive character that she convinced her father, a dyed-in-the-wool Illinois Republican, to campaign for her husband more than once.

Hillary Rodham Clinton is a fine trial lawyer. Before she withdrew from practice, she was making more money in the legal profession than her husband earned. She thoroughly understands the world of adversary relationships. It is clear she enjoys a good fight. She says the long "White Water" legal battles drained her, but, at no time, was she as angry as when it was suggested that she plead guilty to a minor charge and let her husband pardon her. Kenneth Starr would have to prove every single line of every single allegation against her. If necessary, she would be in court until hell freezes over to prove her innocence. In the end, the investigation proved nothing, at least concerning Hillary. The Special Prosecutor went after her husband on matters that were not even related to "White Water."

"History" in the title is well-placed. In the 33 chapters up to "August 1998," you are on a whirlwind tour of Arkansas, Europe, China, Ireland, and even Mongolia. The book could easily be read for its historical content alone. Hillary Rodham Clinton is unique in that she is one of few people in the world to have participated in two attempts to impeach an American President. She made a special study of the Johnson attempt. She participated in the Nixon attempt and was consulted in the attempt to impeach her husband. Her views on the role of impeachment in this country should be given special weight.

Many will read this book primarily to find out why she did not "throw the bum out." She makes it plain that she considered that course of action. She was a betrayed and angry wife, but she was also a betrayed political partner and a disappointed legal partner. What she says and does in Chapter 34 is only comprehensible when you remember the previous 33 chapters of her life. If this were fiction, she would probably have built more suspense into the text before confronting her readers with this vivid scene. But this was life, political life at that, and sometimes things break suddenly in that world.

There is ample evidence in this book that this lady does her homework and reaches her own conclusions. That is especially true in matters of welfare reform and on a myriad of issues relating to women and children. On occasion, those conclusions were not the same as those reached by President Clinton; but she stood her ground and argued them anyway. Did she write this book with a view to running for the Presidency? Probably, but you also get the very clear idea she would have run for major public office much sooner had she not been married to the Bill Clinton. Bottom line: you cannot separate the lawyer from the politician or from the woman. That, in some respects, is the whole point of the book. Every woman is a kaleidoscope. It would be a less interesting world if they were not.

Sadly, not many Republicans will read this book. Many years ago, when Barry Goldwater wrote his *Conscience of a Conservative*, many Democrats read his book and profited from it. Now, we will not even listen to what one another has to say, let alone spend twenty-eight bucks on the book. We will live to regret that narrow-minded point of view.

Clinton's Autobiography

On July 15th in the *Pantagraph's* "Your Views," John Michael launched into a diatribe against the 42nd President of the United States. One might have let it pass, but President Clinton's sterling performance at the Democratic National Convention will not permit that. Having never read his autobiography, Mr. Michael apparently believes, as does President Bush, that it is not really necessary to read books. If he had read the book, he would have discovered the following information. On draft dodging: Clinton had himself declared 1A after he returned from the Rhodes Scholarship to Oxford. He was never called, because his lottery number was too high. White Water: neither he nor his wife was convicted because there was insufficient evidence. Smoking dope: yes, he did that in England. He never did that in the United States; hence, he broke no laws in this country. Ignore terrorists: he established a special unit on terrorism. In his obligatory discussion with the incoming President, he specifically said that he thought the leading problem in George W's Administration would be terrorism. "W" chose not to respond.

On the 177 acts of clemency: actually it was 456 acts, putting him only 50 more than President Reagan. Granting himself immunity: he never did that. Cornering women in the oval office: yes, it was one woman. Some of us still believe that she offered and he accepted.

Pay to hear him speak: certainly. Some of us wish to learn that on many economic indicators the period from 1992 to 2000 (Clinton) was a lot better than the period from 2000 to 2004 (Bush). We heard that same record recited by Clinton, Kennedy, Obama, Edwards, and Kerry, at the Convention. But I am sure that Mr. Michael was not listening.

Hundreds of members of the American Bar Association signed a petition saying that the President's actions, however immoral they may have been, did NOT meet the standard of a "high crime and misdemeanor" as required by the Constitution. Of course, Mr. Michael would not have read that either.

Alexander Hamilton

Ron Chernow's seven-hundred-page biography of one of the most controversial of America's founding fathers can be intimidating reading. But it is worth the effort. Well written, it will hold your attention almost as well as most novels can. Indeed, Alexander Hamilton's life is so adventurous, romantic, gallant, and finally tragic that, were it not so well-documented, one would almost take it for a novel rather than real life. If the screen rights have not already been sold on this book, I will miss my bet.

Of course, this is not the first biography of the youngest of the founding fathers. However, the scholarly detail here is greater than in some of the others. In particular, the work that went into casting light on Hamilton's early life in the West Indies is remarkable. For good reasons, Hamilton chose to obfuscate his origins. His critics called him "the bastard son of a Scotch peddler"; that was not far off the mark. His French Huguenot mother would, in Victorian terms, be fairly described as a "loose woman." His father was the ne'r-do-well, fourth son of a minor Scottish Laird. Hamilton was a very bright lad, so the local citizenry took up a collection to send him to the United States for an education.

Chernow describes his meteoric advance in the Continental Army. Still in his early twenties, he left his studies in King's College (later Columbia University) and raised a company for service in the Revolutionary War. Within almost no time, he had moved from Captain to Lt. Colonel and became George Washington's aide-de-camp. As the war progressed, he became, in reality, Washington's Chief of Staff, although he never possessed the rank that normally goes with such a position. Ultimately, with the exception of the Marquis de Lafayette, he was the youngest senior officer to fight in the American Revolution.

Hamilton was also the youngest man to attend the Constitutional Convention as a delegate from his adopted State of New York. His polished and articulate speeches impressed a group of men who had "heard it all" and would be very difficult to impress. However, his ideas for government were not acceptable to the Convention. Hamilton, like many Conservatives, had a very low opinion of the masses; indeed, he feared the mobs and thought most democracies would end in tyranny. His notions of a Presidency-for-life and a hereditary Senate looked far too much like the British system, which had just been overturned by the sword.

When Washington was elected President, he took his former aide-de-camp into the government with him. Very quickly, Hamilton became Secretary of the Treasury and a major leader in the Federalist Party. He led the opposition to Thomas Jefferson's party and supported the man who later took his life, Aaron Burr. Indeed Chernow is at his best in describing the politics of the early Republic. If you think recent elections have been dirty, you need to reacquaint yourself with the elections of 1800 and 1804.

The politics of the early Republic were personal as well as ideological. Therefore, opponents' sex lives were open to discovery as much as any other facets of their lives. Neither Hamilton nor Burr could pass muster with the "born again Christians" of today. In fact, Hamilton was forced to admit in print at least one of his adulterous adventures.

On the ideological side, Chernow also provides a most valuable service. Much has been written on the effect of the American Revolution on the later French Revolution. However, not nearly enough has been written of the effect of the French Revolution on the early politics of the United States. Chernow helps to redress that imbalance. Many Federalists actually believed that the Jeffersonians were preparing to invite a French army to the United States to overthrow the existing government. The purpose of the invasion would be to establish a government along the lines of the Jacobins then ruling France, replete with a "reign of terror." Indeed, Hamilton raised an army to resist just such a French invasion and then had himself created a Major General and second-in-command. Washington came out of retirement to command this army, but there is some question as to whether or not he actually assumed command. When the danger of war passed, this army was disbanded much to Hamilton's sorrow. Ever after, in the eyes of the Jeffersonians, Hamilton looked suspiciously like a would-be Napoleon.

Finally Chernow takes you slowly step by step through the Byzantine labyrinths of the "code duello" toward that fateful day in Weehawken, New Jersey. He makes a good case for the position that Hamilton may have committed suicide by deliberately throwing his first shot away, although he also shows you that there is no way to absolutely prove this allegation. Chernow also ties up loose ends by telling you what happened to the widow and some of Hamilton's many children, at least the legal ones, after his death.

There can be little doubt that this is excellent biography. Whether it is also good history is a more complex question. It is certainly in the "revisionist" tradition and no one emerges from Chernow's treatment without a lot of scars and blemishes, not even George Washington. The current Thomas Jefferson detractors will find lots of red meat here for their efforts to pull down the third President of the United States. The second President, John Adams, comes off looking like a crank and a neurotic. Perhaps he was. It is surely difficult to understand Adam's absences of up to seven months from Washington while he was President.

This is a book the "neo-conservatives" will cherish. This is a book Liberals will not like. But this is also an honest book, and it deserves your patronage.

Section IX

"Oh, ye'll take the high road and I'll take the low road,
And I'll be in Scotland afore ye."

—On the Bonny Bonny Banks of Loch Loman

IX. Scotland

A. British Politics: Another View

B. When Scot Fought Scot: The American Revolution

C. Tartan Day

British Politics: Another View

In the June 11th issue of the *Pantagraph*, noted columnist, George Will, offers his interpretation of the recent British election and his prognostications for the British election of 2005. But he sees the facts through conservative glasses. Since the Conservatives have been soundly trounced in two successive elections, he sees a revival of the Conservative and Unionist Party in 2006. He may be right, because British politics, like American politics, shows the same pendulum-like swings that occur through time between the Liberal and Conservative poles on the political spectrum. However, another interpretation is possible. The political party gaining the most seats in the most recent British election was the Liberal Democrats, whose gain of six seats puts them at 50 in the House of Commons. This is not many, to be sure, but a look at what is happening in Scotland may suggest a very important role for them in 2005.

In Scotland, Labor governs, but only because of a coalition government which includes the Liberal Democrats. Without them, Labor would not have enough votes to form a government in Scotland. The Liberal Democrats in Scotland have cashed in big on their deal with Labor. Two important social programs, the removal of tuition in higher education and the program for the care of the elderly, have been passed and paid for by increased taxation. Those programs and the increase in taxes necessary to pay for them were the price exacted by the Liberal Democrats for participation in the Lab-Lib coalition.

Could this same scenario develop in the Westminster Parliament by 2005? Yes, it could.* The last poll conducted by the *London Times* showed only 30% of the electorate supporting the Conservative Party.

Admittedly, this is more than the meager 16% who support that same party in Scotland. The Conservative showing in this last election was so bad that both Hague, the U.K. Conservative leader, and Robertson, the Scot Conservative leader, had to resign. Charles Kennedy, the new Liberal Democrat leader, launched a powerful campaign with a plan for revising and expanding a number of social programs, including the National Health Service. Kennedy is a Scot and frequently uses the success of the Liberal Democrats north of the border as an example of what can be done in England. One of his slogans is, "We are the party of opposition now and we will be the party of governance in another ten years."

Mr. Will overlooks the important fact that European politics are often a matter of multi-party coalitions. You cannot make the same two party assumptions in Europe that you do in the United States. A Lab-Lib coalition governs Scotland now and a Lab-Lib coalition could govern England in 2005 or 2011. All right, that's looking at the same subject through liberal glasses rather than through conservative glasses. Now, you look at it through your own glasses.

*[Editorial Note: It could, but it did not. In 2005, the Labor majority was reduced, but not to the point where it needed to form a coalition with the Liberal Party in England.]

When Scot Fought Scot: The American Revolution

Americans of Scottish descent generally understand that, in the American Revolutionary War, the Highland Scots remained loyal to the British Crown, while the "Scotch-Irish" flocked to the standards of George Washington and the Rebels. The battle of Moore's Creek was virtually an all-Scottish affair with the Scotch-Irish gaining a resounding victory over the Highland loyalists. However, many Americans of Scottish ancestry have often wondered why this was the case. After all, Culloden took place only 31 years before Lexington/Concord. Among Highland families the butchery of Lord Cumberland still must have been a vivid memory.

Comes now Michel Newton with his careful study: *We're Indians for Sure Enough: The Legacy of the Scottish Highlanders in the United States*, which is a sequel to his *A Handbook of the Scottish Gaelic World*. Professor Newton, who holds a PhD in Celtic Studies from the University of Edinburgh, has a masterful command of the Scot Gaelic, which enables him to inspect important manuscripts not available to those who do not have the Gaelic language.

With this advantage, it is clear to see that the Highland Scots and the Scotch-Irish were of entirely different cultures and backgrounds. The Scotch-Irish had been driven out of Ulster in the very early part of the 18th Century and they hated the Hanoverian Crown for that reason. A Hessian officer commenting on this state of affairs said, "Count not this an American Revolution. Count this rather a Scotch-Irish Revolution." Inspection of the Pennsylvania Line in Washington's Army reveals at least half of the names are Scotch-Irish in derivation. Clearly, the Scotch-Irish of the Pennsylvania hill country thought that simply another George had come to persecute them, as other Georges had persecuted their grandfathers.

The view from the Highland side was quite different. After Culloden, the British Crown had raised numerous regiments in the Highlands with promises of land in America for those that would serve there. This was a familiar way of life for the Highlander whose ancestors had always "gone to be a soldier." To hold land in turn for military service ("sword land") was a way of life for them. But as Newton makes clear, it was more than simply the promise of land that held them loyal to the Crown. The Highlanders despised Lowlanders, their language and their way of life. The difference between the Galltachd and the Gaidhealtachd was enormous. Differences in speech, in dress, in religion, in diet and in politics were conspicuous. This difference is not present in the modern world. Only through a careful study of the Scot Gaelic can the differences in that older world be revealed.

Still, in the Carolinas of the late 18th Century there were divided loyalties within a single family. Newton recounts the differences between General MacDonald and his son. The General stayed loyal, but his son went with the Patriots. One must not overdo the divisions of the past. The kilts, the highland games, the haggis and all the rest are national customs and costumes of ALL of Scotland. When Newton attacks the Scottish "kitsch" of tartans, bagpipes and the like, he does not appear to fully understand this. To be sure, one could wish that more "want-to-be" Scots would learn the Scot Gaelic. Some are doing exactly that. However, capturing a pure cultural breeze from the Highlands may be beyond the capacity of many an honest Scot ethnic.

Tartan Day

Some years ago, the Congress of the United States declared April 6th to be "Tartan Day." Those of Scottish heritage and those interested in Scotland hoped it would catch on, as has St. Patrick's Day in the United States. It has not done so, but loyal groups of Scots do gather on that day around the country. On this last April 6th, you could have found them at Mollie Miley's Pub in Normal.

On that day, it is obligatory to read the Declaration of Arbroath. April 6, 1320, the nobility of Scotland addressed a petition to Pope John XXII. After detailing their suffering under King Edward I of England and their deliverance from that suffering by Robert the Bruce, they pleaded for recognition of Bruce as King of Scots. He had been King for fifteen years prior to the petition, but had never been recognized as such by the Papacy. This was long before the Reformation. The legitimacy of a King rested strongly on recognition by the Pope.

There are many stirring passages in this document; the Scots do have a flair for the dramatic. One of the most quoted passages follows:

".....for, as long as but a hundred of us remain alive, never will we on any conditions be brought under English rule. It is in truth not for glory, nor riches, nor honours that we fight, but for freedom—for that alone, which no honest man gives up but with life itself."

The original document was in Latin, but even granting some liberality in the English translation, this is indeed a very early statement for freedom and liberty. It would be at least three centuries before notions of freedom ran that high among the English. This tallies with the fact that William Wallace had led a primarily peasant army to oppose

Edward I. His betrayal was largely by the nobility in Scotland who were afraid of this growing national spirit in the peasantry.

So, next April 6th, grab your tartan and join the Scots. You will probably find some of them at Mollie Miley's Pub, still celebrating.

Section X

X. Miscellaneous

Canada

"Oh, Canada, we stand on guard for thee." Well, maybe I don't have to sing the national anthem, but I do need to say some nice things about our northern neighbor. First, the moment you step over the line, your dollar buys one third more than it does in Illinois. That exchange rate is tough on Canadians who like to spend the winter in Florida, but it is a bonanza to us Yanks.* Second, the accommodations and food are fully as good and, in some cases, better than in Illinois. Third, they are most hospitable people. My wife and I must travel now in wheelchairs, when we do our airline business. In the U.S., the attitude seems to be: "Yes, we know we are required by law to provide this service, but we would really rather you handicapped people would not darken our doors again." It could be this is also part of a different attitude toward older people in Canada. Whatever it is, an older person traveling in a wheelchair can expect far better service than they receive here in Illinois. If you are traveling on Air Canada, this service is free. Try not tipping a wheelchair pusher in the U.S. and, brother, you will be sitting in that chair a long, long time.

If you are going on holiday, as my wife and I do to escape the flat land and the endless monotony of the prairie, you will find what you want in Canada. Maritime Canada has the grandest views of the ocean. Whether it is New Brunswick, Prince Edward Island, or Nova Scotia in the east, or British Columbia in the west, the seascapes are exceptional. For example, see Cape North off the Cabot Trail and Peggy's Lighthouse. Try spending some time on a four-rigged schooner or on a lobster boat. They are inspected by the Canadian Coast Guard. Lobster lovers take note of this. One evening, my wife and I dined on lobsters that were taken that morning, in a lobster boat, which we then used for whale watching in the afternoon. The cost: $7.50 US for a pound and a quarter (chicken) lobster. By the way, we sighted fifteen whales on that trip, some within 30 feet of the boat—mostly Minke Whales that run to seven tons and twenty-five feet. If you get there when the "fiddlehead fern" is in season you will have an additional culinary treat.

Is there any downside to all this? Sure. The "black flies," vicious little equivalents to the American mosquito and the Scottish "midge," are bad near the water. But on a day with the wind blowing (and there are lots of those) the little devils will be grounded. Also, there is a touch of guilt. You are helping the Canadian economy, not the American economy, by your little trip north of the border.* Oh well, we did burn the city of Toronto in the war of 1812; maybe we owe this to them?

*[Editorial Note: Less so now since the policies of the Bush Administration have driven the dollar down relative to other currencies.]

Flying the Stars and Bars

The display of the Confederate Flag at public events presents a problem. That is especially true for those of us of the Liberal persuasion. In recent times, the Stars and Bars have been utilized by hate groups and racial supremacy types whose views are anathemas not only to Liberals, but also to many Conservatives. It would be an easy course of action to say, "Burn the damn thing." Did not the Civil War settled what that flag stood for? That would be wrong.

First of all, flying that flag may be covered by the First Amendment of the U.S. Constitution. Even if what it stands for now is distasteful to most, the display of any flag may be a part of free speech being advanced for a cause. The remedy is not to ban flying a flag. The remedy is to fly a flag that symbolizes your beliefs or that advances your cause.

Second, for most of those who served under that flag, the issue was not racial superiority. My maternal Great Granduncle rode with Nathan Bedford Forrest, but he never owned a slave. For him, and countless other Southerners, the issue was liberty and freedom. In my Great Granduncle's view, Lincoln intended to destroy the Constitution and the rights of state governments. When one of Forrest's troopers was asked why he fought so hard he replied, "Because YOU are down HERE." Uncle Will was a Texan. Nobody, but nobody, was going to march an Army across HIS backyard.

Sadly, the Lost Cause was also the Wrong Cause. A southern victory would have been disastrous for this nation. My paternal Great Granduncle, saw that, and followed Sherman to the sea. You grow to respect the people you fight. I believe that the uncle who served in the 37th Indiana Volunteers would want me to support the showing of the

Stars and Bars. After all, nearly two million of his fellow Americans, wrongfully or not, shed their blood for it.

What Do the Masons Stand for?

The Order of Freemasons claims origin from the building of King Solomon's Temple, but written records of the Lodge exist only from the 17th Century in England and Scotland. It is clear that the Lodge developed and expanded in the same 17th Century ferment that activated the Puritans to leave England and to come to the United States seeking religious liberty. In both the American Revolution and the French Revolution, Masons were active in the struggle to establish religious freedom and liberty. Evidence suggests that the plan for the Boston Tea Party may have been hatched in a tavern where the Masonic Lodge usually met. As is well known, General Washington was a Mason. Lodges were definitely held in the Continental Army. French Masons took a leading role in the French Revolution. During the post revolutionary period, French Masons were active in revolutionary movements of the 1820s and 1840s.

In more modern times, the wearing of the familiar triangular symbol with a letter G in the middle of it would buy the wearer a quick trip to one of Hitler's concentration camps. The same was true in Franco's Spain and Mussolini's Italy. To avoid this, during WWII, a small rosette was worn in the lapel in place of the more familiar Masonic emblem. The need for secret recognition signs and signals rose partially from these more violent periods of history. Masons are seldom secretive about what they teach, but there have been periods in which they had to be secretive about who they were.

Students of the history of the order will quickly point out that Masons also supported the King and that many of the "chivalric" degrees may derive from Jacobite connections. When the Bonnie

Dundee fell at the battle of Kilcankee, he allegedly had on his body the cross of a Knight Templar. Likewise, there were lodges within the British Army in the America Revolutionary War. A case can be made that the Prince Hall Masons spring from that source. It is also true that British Masons broke connections with their French brethren over their activities in the French Revolution and in the upheavals of the 19th Century in France. Yes, collaborators with the Fascists did include some Masons. However, we think the weight of historical evidence indicates much more support for freedom of religion and for the basic liberties that underlie religious choice than for the establishment of a state religion and the persecution of heretics.

If the case for support of religious freedom is controvertible, the case for religious tolerance is straightforward. Religious tolerance is built directly into the ritual. The Entered Apprentice is told immediately that he can take his vows on any religious text of his choice, as long as his religion acknowledges the existence of a single God; that is, as long as it is Deistic. For the Christian that is normally the *Bible*. It could be the *Book of Mormon*. For the Jew, it is the *Torah*; for the Muslim it is the *Koran*; for others it could be the *Zid-Avesta*, the *Analects* of Confucius, etc. From the very initial instance of his Masonic existence, the individual is thus confronted with choice and is not commanded to take a single road. This lesson is taught again in the Knight of St. Andrew degree of the Scottish Rite.

It is true that most of the "appendent degrees" in Masonry are designed with the Christian in mind. The upper degrees of both the Scottish and the York Rite might be uncomfortable for non-Christians. That is especially true of the Knight Templar degree, which would seem to require not only a Christian belief, but also a Trinitarian Christian belief. The Royal Order of Scotland also states that none but Christians need apply. Still, in all these appended degrees the non-Christian religion is treated with the utmost respect and courtesy. Even in the Knight Templar degree, the emphasis is not upon the Crusades, but upon the peaceful conclusion of the Crusades. The lesson is one of tolerance toward the Islamic world. The tradition of jihad, holy war, so important to the fundamentalist wing of the Islamic world, has no place in modern Masonry. It is interesting, in this connection, that when the Knights Templar were excommunicated by the Pope, one of the charges was that the Knights engaged in too friendly a relationship with their Muslim counterparts, to the point of practicing heretical rituals and holding heretical beliefs. The point is that, after centuries of warfare, the Templar Knights, themselves, had moved on to belief in religious tolerance. Unfortunately, some of their Muslim adversaries never made that leap forward. Perhaps, they still have not today.

Religious fundamentalists of today, whether of the Christian or the Islamic nature, have trouble with the principle of religious toleration. Bin Laden and the terrorists would simply bomb us out of existence. The Christian fundamentalists are not nearly so bloodthirsty. They would rely on tearing down the barrier between the church and state so carefully created by Thomas Jefferson and his colleagues, many of whom were Masons. They would then proceed to construct a state religion along the lines of their own beliefs and the rest of us would have to conform or face penalties. In short, the fundamentalists would roll us right back to the 17th and 18th Centuries when the Lodge was struggling to establish religious freedom and religious toleration. I, for one, do not want to go back down that path to another Dark Age. The modern Masonic Lodge may stand for many things, but in my humble opinion, they stand tallest and proudest when they stand for religious freedom and religious toleration. The problem is that not enough people know this.

National Treasure and the Masonic Lodge

National Treasure, an adventure film staring Nicolas Cage, has been released in DVD format. I am no movie critic, but it seems to me that this is an acceptable lower-budget film of the type of *Raiders of the Lost Ark*. Members of the Masonic Order may find this film more entertaining than others. The film was made with consultation and assistance of several Masonic bodies. It is based on the legend of the *Lost Treasure of the Knights Templar*. There must be at least two score of books concerning this lost treasure. There are two versions of this legend. One might be called the "standard version" and the other, the "practical version."

The standard version goes something like this. In 1307, Phillipe IV of France and Clement IV, Pope of Rome, attempted to destroy the Knights Templar. This particular group of Knights had been established during the Crusades to protect Christians who were making pilgrimages to Jerusalem, which had been liberated from Saracen rule. For this arduous duty, they had been paid very well and given wide powers within the Catholic Church. They reported directly to the Pope with no intermediaries. By the beginning of the 14th Century, they had several thousand commandaries established all over Europe.

Like most early medieval kings, Phillipe Le Bel was broke. The Knights looked like easy pickings. This was a low point in the affairs of the Papacy. The Popes were imprisoned in a French city and Clement IV was, in effect, the puppet of the French King. So, in late 1307, the King sprang his trap and caught about 600 of the order. At least twice that number escaped, probably with advance warning. The fortunate reached their own fleet of ships in several French ports. The important part is that they took their treasures with them. This was no ordinary treasure. The Knights held the Temple of Solomon as their primary fortification and engaged in a lot of digging in the process. The legend holds that in the process of digging the Knights uncovered the treasury of Solomon, including riches from before the Roman conquests of that part of the world.

Where did the Templar treasure fleet go? To Spain, where they took the title of Knights of Christ and survived for several centuries. They also went to Scotland where they came under the protection of Prince Henry St. Clair. Prince Henry did not believe that Scotland was safe enough for so vast a treasure, so he moved at least a part of it to Nova Scotia and buried it in a "Money Pit" on the east coast of that Canadian province. You can imagine how many holes have been dug in Nova Scotia looking for that treasure right up until today.

The part left in Scotland may have been buried in or around Roslyn Chapel. Roslyn was the holding of the St. Clair, which became the Sinclair, family. If the Masonic Order has anything like a "Holy of Holies," this is it. The entire structure, both inside and outside, is covered with elaborate stone carvings including many Masonic symbols. Among these carvings are some which surely look like ears of corn. Maize or Indian corn was not known in Scotland until centuries later, when it was brought back from the New World. Therefore, the Scots believe that Prince Henry and his sailors got to America long before Christopher Columbus. The movie *National Treasure* builds on this and would have you believe that part of the treasure was buried in Philadelphia.

The "practical" approach to the legend requires you to look closely at the nature of the Knights Templar in the years just prior to their fall. Imagine a merchant in Paris who owes money to another merchant somewhere in the Near East. He cannot just wire money from his bank to another bank. There are no wires and there are no banks. Enter the Knights with their thousands of commandaries throughout the known-world. The Knights have a fearful battle reputation and can safely move gold over long distances. They are a hard drinking lot and they do not smell too good, but their credit is as good as gold. In reality, their "treasure" is marks in accounting books. They are bankers, in other words.

I have visited Knight Templar ruins in northern Belgium. They look like fortified counting houses. Like all bankers, they would have had to have "reserves" in hard metal to back up their paper markers. So, "treasures" may well exist that are yet to be found, but nothing like the enormous hoard of golden statues that the movie finally shows you in its closing scenes. So, you have a choice. Will it be the esoteric riches of the ancient East or will it be Banking 101? I think you know the answer.

The Rational and the Emotional

I had been around the American Educational Finance Association (AEFA) for a very long time. I was there when AEFA was founded; I served as their tenth President; and I received their Distinguished Service award. I was accustomed to being regarded as one of the "Founding Fathers" of that national organization. That was the rational part of being a septuagenarian. The emotional part occurred a few years ago when attending a national conference of AEFA. An attractive young female graduate student got on the crowded elevator with my wife and me, looked at my nametag, and said in a loud voice, "My God, you are Alan Hickrod. I thought you were dead. Why, you are a living legend." There was a burst of laughter from everyone in the elevator. I looked at my wife, Marcia, for support. She only smiled and nodded. It was right then and there that the emotional part of being a septuagenarian took hold. It was not a pleasant feeling. *Sic transit Gloria mundi.*

A Last Word

By the dawn of the 21st Century, the private enterprise system had proven itself more economically efficient than the centralized planned economy. Unfortunately, at least in the United Kingdom and in the United States, history has also shown that if left uncontrolled and unregulated, the private enterprise system will produce great inequalities in income and in wealth. These inequalities permeate through the entire structure of society especially into the educational system and, in the United States, into the system for financing education.

In these essays, we have maintained that it is the central responsibility of Liberalism to cushion and to contain these inequalities. If this is not done, eventually the over-concentration of wealth will destroy the private enterprise system through monopoly and oligopoly. More importantly, an over concentration of wealth is not consistent with democracy and representative government and, if unchecked, will lead to an oligarchy or a plutocracy.

We have also argued that a central pillar of Liberalism is tolerance for other peoples' systems of government and for other peoples' systems of religion. An imperial foreign policy based on "our way or the highway" is very dangerous to this Republic. History is strewn with the wrecks of ships of state than have overreached themselves and foundered on the rocks of hubris. History is also replete with the skeletons of intolerant theocracies.

Hubert Humphrey was correct in observing that each generation must write its own definition of Liberalism. But we contend that no matter which generation writes that definition, opposition to great inequalities and support of tolerance will be central to that definition. So may it ever be.

[Editorial Note: As this publication was in press this splendid book came to hand: Robert B. Reich. *Reason: Why Liberals Will Win the Battle for America*. NY: Vintage Books. 2005. We can honestly say that if you enjoyed this little book, you will be carried away by Professor Reich's effort.]

References

Aristotle. *On Man in the Universe*. New York: Classics Club, Black Inc.. 1943.

Arrow, Kenneth; Bowles, Samuel; and Durlauf, Steven (eds). *Meritocracy and Economic Inequality*. Princeton University Press. 2000.

Byrd, Robert C. *Losing America*. W.W. Norton. 2004.

Chernow, Ron. *Alexander Hamilton*. New York: Penguin. 2000.

Clark, Richard A. *Against All Enemies*. New York: Free Press. 2004.

Clinton, William J. *My Life*. New York: Knopf. 2004.

Clinton, Hillary Rodman. *Living History*. New York: Simon and Schuster. 2004.

Cuomo, Mario M. *Why Lincoln Matters*. New York: Harcourt. 2004.

Dean, John W. *Worse Than Watergate*. New York: Little, Brown, and Co. 2004.

Florida, Richard. *The Rise of the Creative Class*. New York: Basic Book. 2002.

Florida, Richard. *The Flight of the Creative Class*. New York: Harper Collins. 2005.

Frank, Robert H. and Phillip J. Cook. *The Winner Take All Society*. New York: Free Press. 1995

Frank, Thomas. *What's the Matter with Kansas?* New York: Henry Holt. 2004.

Friedman, Thomas L. *The World Is Flat*. New York: Farrar, Straus and Giroux. 2005

Gates, William H., Sr. and Collins, Chuck. *Wealth and Our Commonwealth*. Boston: Beacon Press. 2002.

Galbraith, John Kenneth. *The Affluent Society*. Boston: Houghton Mifflin. 1958.

Galbraith, John Kenneth. *Name Dropping: From FDR On*. Boston: Houghton Mifflin. 1999.

Greider, William. "Galbraith: An Appreciation." *The Nation*. March 14, 2005

Hansen, Gerry, and Fraser. *The Political Guide to Modern Scotland*. London: Politico's Publishing. 2004.

Hartz, Louis. *The Liberal Tradition in America*. New York: Harcourt Brace. 1955.

Hodgson, Godfrey. *More Equal Than Others*. Princeton University Press. 2004.

Huffington, Arianna. *Fanatics and Fools*. New York: Harper. 1992.

Humphrey, Hubert H. *The Cause Is Mankind*. New York: Praeger. 1964.

Huntington, Samuel P. *The Clash of Civilizations*. New York: Simon and Schuster. 1996.

Huntington, Samuel P. *Who Are We?* New York: Simon and Schuster. 2004

Ivins, Molly and Lou Dubose. *Bushwhacked*. New York: Random House. 2003.

Jefferson, Thomas. *Writings*. New York: Penguin. 1984.

Kahlenberg, Richard D. *All Together Now*. Washington, D.C.: Brookings Institute Press. 2001.

Keillor, Garrison. *Homegrown Democrat*. New York: Viking. 2004.

Kozel, Jonathan. *Savage Inequalities: Children in America's Schools*. New York: Harper. 1992

Krugman, Paul. *The Great Unraveling*. New York: W.W. Norton. 2003.

Krugman, Paul. *Fuzzy Math*. New York: W.W. Norton. 2002.

Lazare, Daniel. *The Velvet Coup*. London: Verso. 2001.

Maisel, L. Sandy and Buckley, Kara Z. *Parties and Elections in America*. New York: Roman and Littlefield. 2004.

Micklewait, John and Wooldridge, Adrian. *The Right Nation: Conservative Power in America*. New York: Penguin. 2004.

Mishel, Lawrence; Bernstein, Jared; and Boushey. *The State of Working America*. Cornell University Press. 2003

Newton, Michael. *A Handbook of the Scottish Gaelic World*. Four Courts Press. 2000.

Newton, Michael. *We're Indians for Sure Enough: The Legacy of the Scottish Highlanders in the United States*. Saora Media. 2001.

Parker, Richard. *John Kenneth Galbraith: His Life, His Politics, and His Economics*. New York: Farrar, Strauss and Giroux. 2004

Phillips, Kevin. *Wealth and Democracy*. New York: Broadway Books. 2004.

Phillips, Kevin. *American Dynasty*. New York: Viking. 2004

Popper, Karl. *The Open Society and Its Enemies*. London: Routledge. 1945.

Rawls, John. *Political Liberalism*. Columbia University Press. 1996.

Reitan, Earl A. *Liberalism: Time Tested Principles for the Twenty First Century*. Lincoln, NE: iUniverse. 2004.

Reitan, Earl A. *Time Is/Time Was/Time Never More Shall Be*. Normal, IL: Babbitt's Books. 2005.

Rifkin, Jeremy. *The European Dream*, New York: Tarcher/Penquin. 2004.

Roosevelt, Theodore. *Autobiography*. New York: Da Capo Press. 1913.

Roskin, Marcus G. *Liberalism: The Genius of American Ideals*. Lanham, MD: Rowman and Littlefield. 2004.

Rothstein, Richard. *Class and Schools*. Washington, DC: Economic Policy Institute. 2004.

Ryscavage, Paul. *Income Inequality in America*. New York: M.E. Sharpe, 1999.

Sasson, Helen (Ed). Between Friends: *Perspectives on John Kenneth Galbraith*. Boston: Houghton Mifflin. 1999.

Schlessinger, Arthur M., Jr. *A Life in the Twentieth Century*. Boston: Houghton Mifflin, 2000.

Schlessinger, Arthur M., Jr. *War and the American Presidency*. New York: W. W. Norton. 2004.

Schweke, William, *Smart Money, Education and Economic Development*. Washington, DC: Economic Policy Institute. 2004.

Simon, Paul. *Our Culture of Pandering*, Carbondale, IL: Southern Illinois University Press. 2003.

Simon, Paul. *Healing America*. Maryknoll, NY: Orbis Books. 2003.

Sorensen, Theodore (ed). *Let the Word Go Forth: The Speeches of John F. Kennedy, 1947 to 1963*. New York: Delacorte Press. 1988.

Stiefal, Leanna and Others. *Measuring School Performance and Efficiency*. Larchmont, NY: Eye on Education. 2005

Toynbee, Arnold. *A Study of History*. Oxford University Press. 1962.

Trench, Alan. *Has Evolution Made a Difference?* Charlottsville, VA: Imprint Academic Philosophy Documentation Center. 2004

Walter, David. *The Strange Rebirth of Liberal England*. London: Politico's Publishing.

Wessel, David. "As Rich-Poor Gap Widens in the U.S., Class Mobility Stalls." *Wall Street Journal On-Line*. May 13, 2005.

Wolf, Edward N. *Top Heavy*. New York: The New Press. 2002

978-0-595-36861-7
0-595-36861-1